Rabbi Moshe Meir Weiss

on the Yamim Noraim

Powerful guidance for growth and fulfillment

Rabbi Moshe Meir Weiss

on the Yamim Noraim

Powerful guidance for growth and fulfillment

Featuring "40 Days, 40 Ways"
A step-by-step guide to personal improvement

Rabbi Moshe Meir Weiss on the Yamim Noraim
—powerful guidance for growth and fulfillment

© 2007 Rabbi Moshe Meir Weiss

All rights reserved. No part of this publication may be
translated, reproduced, stored in a retrieval system
or transmitted in any form or by any means, electronic,
mechanical, photocopying, recording or otherwise,
without permission in writing from the publisher.

ISBN: 978-1-932443-75-2

Editor: Baila Rosenbaum
Proofreader: Hadassa Goldsmith

THE JUDAICA PRESS, INC.
123 Ditmas Avenue / Brooklyn, NY 11218
718-972-6200 / 800-972-6201
info@judaicapress.com
www.judaicapress.com

Manufactured in the United States of America

Haskama from the Novominsker Rebbe, *shlit"a*

RABBI YAAKOV PERLOW
1569 - 47TH STREET
BROOKLYN N.Y. 11219

יעקב פרלוב
קהל עדת יעקב נאוואמינסק
ישיבת נאוואמינסק - קול יהודא
ברוקלין, נ.י.

Rabbi Moshe Meir Weiss, a prominent Rabbi and Talmud lecturer, has written a very edifying book to help people improve the quality of their lives. It is a work grounded in the eternal values transmitted by the Torah and our revered Sages, and it will certainly serve as an uplifting, practical guide to help Jews attain a more satisfying and rewarding existence.

Yaakov Perlow

HaRav Moshe Feinstein, *zt"l*, wrote this letter on
26 Shevat 5744 in praise of the author, upon his assumption
of the position of Rav of Agudas Yisroel of Staten Island.

RABBI MOSES FEINSTEIN
455 F. D. R. DRIVE
New York, N. Y. 10002

———

ORegon 7-1222

מ ש ה   פ י י נ ש ט י י ן
ר"ם תפארת ירושלים
בנוא יארק

בע"ה

כו׳ שבט תשד"ם

לכבוד קהל אגודת ישראל בסטעטן אייל נד, ה׳ עליהם יחיו.

בשמחה   שמעתי איך שבית הכנסת אגודת ישראל בסטעטן־
איילנד, זכה לקבל לרב ומרא דאתרא את חלמידי היקר
והחביב הרה"ג ר׳ משה מאיר וייס שליט"א – הריני בטוח
שאנשי הקהלה יהנו מאוד מרבנותו של הרה"ג הנ"ל מחמת
מדותיו והנהגותיו הישרים ומחמת ידיעותיו הגדולות
בש"ס ובהלכה, שיועילו לו ליעץ ולעזור אנשי קהלתו בכל
אפשרות שיהיה לו.

ובאתי בזה לברך לתלמידי הרה"ג ר׳ משה מאיר וייס
שליט"א וגם לכל הנהלת וגבאי בית הכנסת וגם לכל חברי
ביהכנ"ס הנ"ל שינהם רבנותו בהצלחה גדולה לתפארת ה׳ ולחורתו
ויזכה ללכת בראש אנשי קהלתו לקבל פני משיח צדקנו בקרוב.

בידידות *אשר בייסן ל*

Haskama from Rav Pam, zt"l, for the author's first sefer.

אברהם פאם
RABBI ABRAHAM PAM
582 EAST SEVENTH STREET
BROOKLYN, NEW YORK 11218

ב"ה מרחשון תשנ"ו

הנה ידי"נ הרה"ג מוהר"ר מאיר וייס שליט"א, חבר ספר הולכן
לבטוח, ראיתי חלפתי וברכת, ועם קראתי ריפ"ף לחכם כזה שנזר ביתו וכבודה,
בדבר חיזוק והתעוררות הדות והמצות כ' ג ג' בעניני אלו
תקנה אל חכר לראשון בענין מוסר, ומתם יד בזר בעניני מתוקן,
ואחרא תני שהמעיינים בו יקבלו ממנו תועלת מאד חשובה ג' וילדר, כי כבר
נועד הוא מחבר לחבלה דבר ממנו הנלבבות ודברים הנאמרים היוצאים מן לב
ונכנסים ללב.

ולכן מברכו כ' חבר ספרו זה בהצלחות חן וחסד בעיני אלקים ואדם
וזכה, ונחמק בריאות הצלע ואמונה דבר ושמחת לב.
אברכם ידיד הכנב ס"ל

לע׳נ האוהב שלום ורודף שלום

דוד יעקב ברוקשטיין, ע׳ה

ד בקה נפשו בבורא יתברך שמו

ו שם שמים היה מתאהב על ידו

ד ברי חכמתו בנחת נשמעו

י דו פרושה לעניים ונצרכים

ע וזר דלים ומחזק נצרכים

ק בע עתים לתורת חיים

ב הצנע לכת עשה משפט וחסדים

ב סבר פנים יפות קיבל כל יצור

נ שא ונתן באמונה וביושר

ח ינך את בניו לתורתו ואהבתו

נ טע יראת שמים בכל משפחתו

ו יעבור את ימי הזעם באמונה בבוראו

כ תב ספר תורה בהידורו

ז כה עם אשתו להשראת שכינתו

י ותר מגופו כיבד את אשתו

נ שא חן בעיני אלקים וכל מכירו

ד מות דיוקנו צדקתו וענוותנותו

ל עולם עטרת ראש של משפחתו

In loving memory of

Jacob & Rose Bruckstein, ע״ה

from their children

Alex & Dorothy Bruckstein

Eliezer & Basya Bruckstein & Family

לע'נ האשה הצנועה

רויזא ברוקשטיין, ע'ה

ר דפה צדקה וחסד בהצנע כל ימיה

ו להחיות לב נדכאים וחולות דרכיה

י וצאי חלציה לומדי תורה ותומכיה

ז כו ללמוד מיראתה וטוהר נשמתה

א ת כיבוד אב ואם קיימה בכל דקדוקיה

ב אהבה חיתה עם בעלה בנועם מדותיה

ת הלים גמרה כל יומים בכוונותיה

א ת שבת קודש כבדה בכל כוחותיה

ל עולי רוסיא עזרה מתוך רחמיה

י פה וטוב היה לה ספר תורה מכל כספיה

ע ברה ימי הזעם באמונה באלוקיה

ז כרה יהיה ברוך עם כל קדושי עמה

ר אשונה היתה לדבר מצוה בכוחותיה

ל שונה דברה אמת כל ימי חייה

י ראת ד' ואהבת חסד נטעה בלב בניה

פ יה פתחה בחכמה כל ימיה

א שת חיל היתה לבעלה ותפארת לבניה

In loving memory of our grandparents

ע״ה Jacob & Rose Bruckstein,

Yitzy & Tammy Roz & Family
Mark & Shavy Schlossberg & Family
Binyamin & Sori Laufer & Family
Moishe Bruckstein

לזכר נשמת

ר' קלונימוס קלמן בן ר' יהודה, ע"ה

ר' מרדכי בן משה הכהן, ע"ה

Dedicated by

Eva & Chaim Silber

רפאנו ה' ונרפא

May Hashem grant a

**רפואה שלמה בקרוב
בתוך שאר חולי ישראל**

to

גדליה מנחם מנדל בן הענא

and

יהושע בן חיה בילה

Dedicated by all their friends who love them

In loving memory of

אברהם בן עזרא ז״ל
Albert Roberts

Dedicated by

Dr. Richard & Devora Roberts

In loving memory of
my Zeide

ר' מנחם בן ר' יצחק ז"ל
Dr. Menachem Yurowitz

who heroically saved his family from the
clutches of the Nazis and built a dynasty
on American shores. His life was dedicated
to Torah, *tefilla b'minyan*, Eretz Yisrael and
the thousands of students whom he helped,
spanning generations, with his vast, masterful
and unparalleled knowledge of speech therapy.
May his *neshama* have an *aliya* from this *sefer*
and may he be a *meilitz yosher* for my mother,
our entire family, and all of Klal Yisrael.

Dedicated by

Rabbi Moshe Meir & Miriam Libby Weiss

נר זכרון

ר' משה בן ר' יהודה לייב הלוי ז"ל
מרת רחל בת ר' יהודה ז"ל

ר' אליעזר בן אברהם לייב ז"ל
מרת רייזל בת ר' אלטר יעקב דוד ז"ל

In loving memory of our beloved
parents, grandparents and great-grandparents
Morris and Ruth Sitzer
Leo and Rose Zachter

ת.נ.צ.ב.ה.

Dedicated by

Mel and Phyllis Zachter
Elie and Cindy Becker
Ephraim, Shani, Shira and Chana Rochel
Yaakov and Elana Zachter
Yehuda and Mindy Zachter
Yitzchak

In loving memory of

**Yosef (Ossie) ben Avrohom Chaim Nuta
Schonfeld,** *zt"l, zy"a,*

who survived the Shoah to build a dynasty
of Torah and mitzvos.

Dedicated by

The Schonfeld families

לעילוי נשמת

דוד לוי בן ישעי' זאב שטרן

סערל בת ישעי' שטרן

ישעי' זאב בן שלמה שטרן

שרה בת חיים אליעזר שטרן

ישעי' בן חיים אליעזר קרויס

אסתר בת משה ארי' קרויס

and all the family who perished during the Holocaust

Dedicated by

The Stern family

Contents

Showing appreciation is a very fitting subject for a sefer on the Yamim Noraim. As we get ready for the day of judgment and take stock of our lives, besides our obvious efforts at petitioning Hashem for a sweet new year, an intelligent person will also use this critical time to say thank you to Hashem for all the blessings of the past year.

In this spirit, echoing the passionate words of Dovid Hamelech, "*Mah ashiv laHashem kol tagmulohi alai*—What can I say to Hashem for all the kindness He has shown me?," I will try to respond with another beautiful expression from Dovid Hamelech: "*Ahal'la Hashem b'chayai; azamra leilokai b'odi*—I offer praise to Hashem with my life, I sing to Hashem while I exist." The Malbim explains that the word "*b'odi*" contains the root word "*od*" which means more or extra. Thus, the intent of the verse is, "I praise Hashem for the basics of life and I offer special praise for all the extras He has given me." I too want to fervently thank Hashem for granting me life and for all the extras, including the exciting gift of being able to offer this new sefer on the Yamim Noraim to Jews throughout the world.

I pray to Hashem that this sefer should find favor in the eyes of the public and motivate them to better themselves, and may Hashem allow me to continue to be *marbitz* Torah to the masses for many years to come.

This is my fourth sefer, *baruch Hashem*, and Judaica Press has published all four. As such, it is obvious that my gratitude to Aryeh Mezei and Mrs. Goldman is overwhelming. (I will never forget her husband Jack, ע״ה, of Otzar Haseforim fame, one of the truly great American publishers.) However, when it comes to this sefer, I am especially indebted to Aryeh. He had totally different plans for the format of this sefer. At the eleventh hour, I marched into his office and requested a total makeover of the project. Instead of telling me to "go jump in a lake," he responded with kindness and acquiescence. Aryeh, I am deeply grateful to you, and wish you and your family much Torah nachas and success.

While it was Aryeh who gave my last-minute request the green light, the burden of all the details and pressures fell squarely on the head of Nachum Shapiro. When I told him how appreciative I was, he responded so beautifully, "It is a pleasure to help a *talmid chacham*." Nachum, may you and Aryeh accomplish many great things together, and may you too have much nachas and happiness with your family.

As a Rav and a twice-daily Daf Yomi Maggid Shiur, it would be quite impossible to successfully write a sefer without the right kind of help. *Baruch Hashem* that I have this kind of assistance from my good friend, Sheldon Zeitlin. Shelley takes dictation from me over the phone and then edits the words into works of art. He is so familiar with my style that he sometimes types the words before they are out of my mouth. Shelley, please know that I couldn't have done it without you, and my appreciation knows no bounds. May Hashem bless you and Estee, together with Ora and Elie, with all of life's blessings.

The job of editing is a meticulous sifting process. I would like to thank Mrs. Baila Rosenbaum for going over the manuscript with a fine-tooth comb and making many improvements.

The seriousness, urgency and spiritual possibilities of the Yamim Noraim that I try to convey in this sefer were born in me during my dozen years in the rarified atmosphere of the Yeshiva of Staten Island. I had the great privilege of spending a decade of Yamim Noraim in the presence of Moreinu V'Rabbeinu HaRav Moshe Feinstein, *zt"l, zy"a*. He called out the one hundred shofar blasts on Rosh Hashanah, filling our hearts with awe. Before Mincha on Yom Kippur, he came in with a long list of people's names categorized according to their needs: some who were ill, others childless, still others needing a shidduch. Seeing this set the tone for us as to what was at stake during this critical time of the year. Also, from the very beginning of Elul, and intensifying as we drew closer to the Day of Judgment, Rabbi Weiss's and Rabbi Mintz's *shmuessen* really motivated us to want to analyze our behavior and motivations and prodded us to change and improve. HaRav Reuven Feinstein, *shlit"a*, the present Rosh Yeshiva, always inspired us with his warmth, pursuit of peace at all costs and his depth of Torah understanding. My *hakaras hatov* to them is deep and sincere, and may Hashem bless them to inspire and motivate many more Talmidim.

Even before my tenure at the Yeshiva, I was invested with the right attitude to the Yamim Noraim growing up in the warm and wonderful home of my parents, Mr. and Mrs. Heshy and Agnes Weiss. They inculcated me with the proper synthesis of values, both *bein adam laMakom*, between man and his Creator, and *bein adam l'chaveiro*, between man and his fellowman. May my father's neshama have an *aliya* in Gan Eden! *L'havdil bein chaim l'chaim*, may my mother, together with her wonderful husband, Mr. Yaakov Goldman (who we affectionately call "Saba") have long life, good health and many years of nachas from us.

Another strong influence in forming my vision and approach to the Yamim Noraim is the Agudas Yisroel of Staten Island Beis Eliezer, where I have been blessed to be the Rav, *b'li ayin hara*, for almost a quarter of a century. The wonderful *baalei tefilla* in our *kehilla*, coupled with many *baal habatim* who diligently join me in an effort to better ourselves, has certainly strengthened and sharpened my perspective toward this holy time of the year. I would like to thank the Agudah for granting me a happy spiritual home for so many years, and may we continue to grow together with harmony and prosperity, learning much Torah and doing many mitzvos until the coming of Mashiach, speedily in our days.

Although my shul is made up of many wonderful and caring people, I would like to single out one extraordinary individual, Reb Shmuel Leifer, my shul's president, who has come through time and time again, helping me navigate the *kehilla* through the sometimes choppy seas that a vibrant shul sometimes experiences.

Actually, one of my most dramatic memories of the Yamim Noraim centers on Reb Shmuel. He works for the Port Authority and was on the seventy-third floor of the First Tower when the plane hit on September 11, 2001. With Hashem's help, he made it out safely. He is our *baal tefilla* for Kol Nidrei. Before he said the *"shehechiyanu"* that evening to thank Hashem for keeping him alive, I poignantly announced to the *kehilla* that I doubt that they will ever hear such an emotional "*shehechiyanu*" as they were about to hear from Reb Shmuel that year. Reb Shmuel, thank you for all you do for us. May your late wife Myrna's neshama have an aliya in Gan Eden, and together with your present *aishes chayil*, Anny, may you be blessed with many years of good health and Torah nachas.

The chapters in this book passed through many stages. Usually the first step is when I prepare to say them at my Tuesday night Hashkafa/Parsha shiur at Rabbi Landau's famous shul in Flatbush. Thank you, Rabbi Landau, for giving me such a wonderful platform, from which I am able to be *marbitz* Torah. May you continue to successfully use your wonderful shul as a springboard for many wonderful projects for many years to come. Special thanks to Mr. Isaacs, who is my right hand man at the shiur. I also wan to thank my devoted audience for coming week after week, and without whom the shiur, of course, would not be possible.

The shiur in Flatbush also serves as a "studio" where I create my weekly tape and CDs that, *baruch Hashem*, go out to several hundred people across the country. I thank with all my heart my devoted "postal Talmidim," who through their subscriptions have made it possible for me to devote myself more thoroughly to *harbatzas Torah* all these years. (If you're interested in joining this weekly "club," the back of this sefer provides information on how to do so.) May Hashem bless us that we share many more years of Torah inspiration together.

After I say the shiur in Flatbush, I develop and refine it further before I share it with my *kehilla* on Shabbos. There, I have many Torah veterans who keep me on my toes with their Torah scholarship. I then get a chance to say the shiur yet from a different angle when I share it with my wonderful *talmidos* at Machon Bais Yaakov Seminary. Thank you, Rebbitzen Steinharter, for putting up with my hectic schedule and giving me this terrific charge of being a *mechaneich* to B'nos Yisroel.

After this refining process, I start to transform my thoughts into the printed word for Yossi Tov, my good friend of many years, who prints them in the *Country Yossi* magazine. Yossi, thanks for being such a solid friend, and may you and yours be blessed with all of life's sweetness.

I also have the tremendous privilege of having a weekly column in *The Jewish Press*. It is with great excitement that I submit my Torah thoughts to them every week, knowing that myriads of people read them across the globe. I want to thank Jerry Greenwald and the many others who play a part in making this happen. Please know that I never take for granted the privilege it is to have your paper as a vehicle for *harbatzas Torah* and *kiddush Hashem*.

I also want to warmly thank Rabbi Eli Teitelbaum, *shlit"a*, for granting me the privilege of airing my shiurim on the Torah communications network Dial-a-Shiur. Rabbi Teitelbaum is one of the great pioneers of mass global *harbatzas Torah* and may Hashem bless him with health and well-being to continue his vital works for many years to come.

During the last few years, with the help of Hashem, I have joined the thrilling and fantastic Kol Haloshon Network. Through this medium, thousands of people have been able to listen to my Daf Yomi, Chumash and Seminary classes. I would like to thank Dovid Panzer, the American

Coordinator of Kol Haloshon, for inviting me to join the rarified ranks of Kol Haloshon. I am greatly in your debt, and may Hashem reward you and your family for all your time and devotion to *harbatzas Torah*. Special thanks also goes to the anonymous London supporter who finances Kol Haloshon and makes it all possible.

The financial kickoff for this sefer came from my good friends Dr. and Mrs. Bruckstein, who dedicated the cover of the sefer as the Bruckstein Edition. May Hashem bless you to always be able to give and never need to take, and may you enjoy good health and Torah blessings for many years to come. Thanks also to Mr. and Mrs. Abe Sprei for financing the expensive equipment for me to be able to mass-produce my Torah CDs. Mr. and Mrs. David Schonfeld also helped me in this vital area.

Thank you also to Mr. and Mrs. Chaim Silber for your constant friendship and support and for being there at just the right time. May Hashem bless you with good health and much nachas from your family. To my personal physician and very dear friend Rabbi Dr. Yitzchok Kurtzer, thank you for being available 24/7! May Hashem bless you and Rochel, together with your wonderful bunch, everything sweet and wonderful. Thank you also to Mr. and Mrs. Mel and Phyllis Zachter, who are always there when we need them. May Hashem bless you in kind for all your many wonderful acts of chesed!

I would like to recognize my Daf Yomi "families," both in Staten Island and Boro Park, that I spend so much Torah time with. Very special thanks to Reb Aaron Finkelstein, who has maintained my Daf Yomi shiur in Boro Park for

Acknowledgments

the last seventeen years! Aaron, please know that the shiur couldn't exist without you! May Hashem grant you and yours much nachas and Torah success.

I would also like to deeply thank my Staten Island Rabbinical colleagues, Rabbi Tzvi Pollack, *shlit"a*, and Rabbi Yaakov Lehrfeld, *shlit"a*. Both are wise friends and allow me to be *marbitz* Torah in their respective *kehillos*. Please know that I am very grateful and may Hashem bless you with the best of everything!

Finally, I would like to express my boundless appreciation to my life's companion Miriam Libby, *tichyeh*. Thank you for supporting me in all my efforts at *harbatzas Torah*. Thank you for staying up many a night to help me mail out the tapes and CDs. Thank you for working your life around my very unusual and trying schedule. May Hashem bless us both with long life and good health to walk all our children and grandchildren down to the chupah, and may we be *zoche* together to see much nachas from them, until the coming of Mashiach speedily in our days!

With Hashem's help,

Moshe Meir Weiss
9 Tammuz 5767

Preface

I am excited that you are reading this sefer. It means that you are joining me on a mission to better your life and be more prepared for the upcoming days of judgment. My fervent prayer to Hashem is that the ideas in this sefer should help us all achieve a healthy, happy and more meaningful new year.

We know that the shofar is blown during the month of Elul as a clarion call to wake us up and stir us to work on ourselves. The *K'sav Sofer* adds that the word *"shofar"* hints at the message, *"shapru maseichem*—improve your ways." With that in mind, this sefer begins with a 40-day program of self-improvement—one separate thought for each of the days from Rosh Chodesh Elul until Yom Kippur, to give you a framework within which to work at this time of the year. Of course, every person is different, so some of us need to work on certain areas more than on others. This list is by no means all encompassing; but it is a start.

I hope that if you find these steps helpful, you will share them with your family at the Shabbos and dinner table. I certainly do not profess to be any sort of expert about the items and goals mentioned here, but I hope to work on them along with you. May you find this mission both inspiring and enjoyable! *Hatzlacha rabbah!*

40 Days, 40 Ways

A Step-by-Step Guide to Personal Improvement

30 Av—Rosh Chodesh Elul

Focus on Hashem as often as possible, for this is the main purpose of life. As Moshe Rabbeinu taught us, "*Mah Hashem Elokecha sho'el ma'imach ki im l'yirah es Hashem Elokecha*—What does Hashem your God ask from you but that you should be aware of Him?" (Devarim 10:12). The Navi Chavakuk echoes this sentiment when he says that we can boil down all of the mitzvos to one essential mission, "*Tzaddik b'emunaso yichyeh*—The righteous person lives with his faith" (Chavakuk 2:4). So, too, does Shlomo Hamelech teach us in his wisdom, "*Sof davar, hakol nishma: Es Elokim yirah v'es mitzvosav sh'mor, ki zeh kol ha'adam*— After everything has been tabulated and heard, be aware of God and heed His commandments, for this is the whole man" (Koheles 12:13). In this vein, we are taught, "*Bechol derachecha da'eihu, v'hu yeyasher orchosecha*—In all of your ways acknowledge Him, and He will keep your path straight" (Mishlei 3:6). This focus is life's essential wisdom, as it says, "*Hein yiras Hashem hi chachmah*—Behold, awareness of Hashem is wisdom" (Iyov 28:28), and it promises us longevity, as it states, "*Yiras Hashem tosif yamim*—Awareness of Hashem adds to one's days" (Mishlei 10:27).

1 Elul—Rosh Chodesh Elul

Concentrate on saying Hashem's Name with kavanah, both in your tefillos and in your brachos. Raise your voice subtly whenever you say Hashem's Name to stir yourself to be more attentive. Focus on the fact that He is everyone's Master, and He was, is and always will be. The rewards of this discipline are great, as it states, *"Bechol hamakom asher azkir es shemi, avo eilecha u'veirachticha*—In every place that you mention my Name, I will come to you and bless you"* (Shemos 20:21).

2 Elul

Thank Hashem often in your prayers and blessings. Remember the mantra of the *Chovos Halevavos*, *"D'varim sherotze l'hasmid bah, al tivtach bah*—Things that you want to continue, don't take for granted." Remember that tefillah is the reason that we were created, as it says, *"Am zu yatzarti li, tihilasi yisapeiru*—I created this nation for Me to relate My praise"* (Yeshaya 43:21). This is the reason we are called *"Yehudim,"* meaning, "the people who give thanks." It is our powerful claim for continued life, as we say in Modim d'Rabbanan, *"Kein t'chaiyeinu u'skay'meinu ... al she'anachnu modim lach*—Continue to grant us life and existence ... for we give thanks to You."

Start your day off right with a fervent *"Modeh ani l'fanecha,"* thanking Hashem for another potentially wonderful day. End the day correctly with Kriyas Shema al Hamita, thereby sandwiching your day with heartfelt thanks to Hashem.

Pay special attention to bentching, remembering that its first three blessings are Biblical in nature. The Chofetz Chaim guarantees us that one who bentches with concentration will be granted his livelihood with dignity and plenty all of his days. When Rav Shach was asked why he merited such longevity, he answered that he always took pains to bentch from a bentcher. Rav Chaim Ozer Grodzensky, too, despite having a photographic memory, also took pains to bentch from a bentcher.

The other Biblical blessing is Birchas HaTorah, the daily blessings over the Torah. Say them with intense appreciation for the gift of Torah, which is our light and guidance in this world and the key to our Eternity, as we say in the blessing, "*V'chaiyei olam nata b'sochienu*—You planted everlasting life in our midst." Ask for the sweetness and enjoyment of Torah for yourself and your progeny with the words, "*v'ha'arev nah*—please make it sweet." Also, give special consideration to the blessing "*asher yatzar es ha'adam b'chachmah*—Who created Man with wisdom," which we say when we come out of the lavatory. Each time you make this blessing, have in mind to thank Hashem for one of the many wonderful gifts Hashem created within you—kidneys, a heart, lungs, a pancreas, a liver, a brain, eyes, vocal chords, ears, teeth, balance, etc. Rav Avigdor Miller recommends making sure to thank Hashem for one specific thing in every "modim" (prayer of thanks) that we say. We must train ourselves to think about this before every Shemoneh Esrei.

3 Elul

Pray for your needs before you are lacking, as the Gemara in *Maseches Shabbos* (32a) advises, "*L'olam y'vakeish adam rachamim shelo yechele*—A person should ask for mercy that he shouldn't become sick." Pray in anticipation and not in reaction. As the friends of Iyov asked him, "*Haya'aroch shuacha lo v'tzar*—Did you arrange your prayers before troubles came?" (Iyov 36:19).

Pray for a good night's sleep in Hashkiveinu, the bracha we say before our Maariv Shemoneh Esrei. Ask for peace of mind, peace at home, peace on the road and peace for Klal Yisrael and Eretz Yisrael in Sim Shalom and Shalom Rav. Pray that Hashem should send us Mashiach and hope for his arrival in the bracha of Es Tzemach Dovid. Pray for protection against homicide bombers, terrorists and people who would subvert our children in the blessing V'lamalshinim Al T'hi Sikva. Ask Hashem to help you to do the mitzvos with passion and meaning when you say, "*v'dabeik libeinu b'mitzvosecha*—attach our hearts to Your mitzvos" in the bracha of Ahavah Rabbah/Ahavas Olam. At the beginning of the week, in the blessing of Atah Chonantanu on Motzaei Shabbos, say fervently the prayer, "*Hacheil aleinu hayamim haba'im likraseinu l'shalom, chasuchim mikol cheit, u'mnukim mikol avon, um'dubakim b'yirasecha*—Start these days that come to greet us in peace, that they should be free of sin and invested with awareness of Hashem."

Always try to daven with a minyan. Realize that one who davens alone might not merit to be heard, but one who davens with a minyan always has an audience with Hashem!

4 Elul

Make *shalom bayis*, marital harmony, one of your top priorities. It should affect all of your major decisions and be constantly on your mind. Live up to the deal you made under the chupah—from that point on, you agreed to make your spouse the most important person in your life. Learn from the sage advice of Rav Yaakov Kamenetsky, *zt"l*, who advised that from the moment of the chupah one should stop thinking in terms of "I" and always think in terms of "we." Rav Chaim Vital stated that the true character of a person can be seen in how they treat their spouse. It is the true barometer of how we synthesize all of the middos that make up a successful Torah personality.

Make sure to express your love and appreciation to your spouse often. Concretize these expressions with gifts, small and large, according to your means. Be warm and caring, courteous and considerate, attentive and affectionate, patient and kind. Take the initiative often to offer to help without needing to be asked. Always remember the following mantra: In marriage, the best way to get something is to give it.

5 Elul

Tell yourself: I will make more of a difference in the lives of my children. I will teach by example, demonstrating in my personal behavior certain critical skills such as how to apologize, compromise and show tolerance, and how to be cheerful, responsible and willing to listen. Most of all, I will demonstrate a constant attention to Torah and mitzvos. I will be mindful of the ever-present opportunity to etch my personal legacy in the lives of my descendants. I will always remember that the best present I can give my children is more of my presence. So, although when I am at the office I am certainly working for their benefit, I can benefit them even more whenever I can get away from work and spend time with them in person.

6 Elul

At every stage of our lives, let's take our responsibility to our parents very seriously. As children, we must listen to them religiously. We should keep in mind that more than anyone else, they have our best interest at heart. As adults, we must respect them and spend time with them often, giving them our attention even though we have so many other demands vying for our time.

The *Kitzur Shulchan Aruch* teaches us that the very best way to give our parents respect is to live righteous lives. Then people will say, "Fortunate are the parents who brought such a child into the world." Even if our parents are already in the Next World, we still have the duty to send them "nachas packages" of our mitzvos and Torah learning. We should pray, from time to time, that their *menucha* should be *b'kavod*, their resting place should be an honorable one in the Next World.

We are taught that there are three partners in the creation of man; namely, the father, the mother and Hashem. Hashem is the silent partner, but He gauges how we would treat Him by how we behave with our parents. Let's make Him proud.

7 Elul

Change is the challenge of life. One must always strive to improve, for we are not rewarded for the raw materials that Hashem gave to us. Motivate yourself to do better so that Hashem does not need to manufacture *nisyonos*, tests, for you. Ask yourself, "Am I a better Jew, spouse, parent, child or friend than I was last year?" Pray in the Shemoneh Esrei blessing of Hashiveinu with intense fervor, "*V'hachazireinu bis'shuvah sh'leimah l'fanecha*—Return us in complete repentance to You."

8 Elul

Think daily about the Afterlife, and invest in it often, for that is what we prepare for in this world. As the Mishnah teaches us, "*Ha'olam hazeh domeh l'prozdor bifnei Olam Habah*—This world is but a corridor before the World to Come" (*Pirkei Avos* 4:16). This world is like the coatroom, while the Afterlife is like the wedding hall. No one travels to Marina Del Ray, for example, just to spend the evening in the coatroom.

9 Elul

In his famous letter to his children (which eventually became known to the entire world and throughout the ages), the first advice of the Ramban is to speak gently to all people and at all times. It is a habit that defines our relationships and affects the outcome of much of our actions. Remember, the mouth is a window to our souls. Let's allow people to take a look at our neshamos and be impressed with what they see. Save your most tender speech for your spouse. You will be rewarded in kind.

10 Elul

Choose the middle path of moderation and shun all that is radical and extreme. It is for this reason that, on every hand, the tallest finger is the middle one while the smallest ones are the pinky and the thumb. The Rambam teaches that the only exceptions to this golden mean are anger and pride, from which we must distance ourselves exceedingly.

11 Elul

From time to time, think about the day you will die and, *Rachmana litzlan*, the possibility of your life suddenly ending. Use this as a powerful motivation not to procrastinate and put off life's essential priorities and goals, such as Torah learning, mitzvos and familial responsibilities.

12 Elul

Cherish the day of Shabbos, for it is one of Hashem's greatest gifts to us. Honor it with fine dress, special care in your speech and slower prayers that are more focused on Hashem than on yourself. As it says, *"Mizmor shir l'yom HaShabbos, tov l'hodos l'Hashem*—A song for the Shabbos day; it is good to thank Hashem" (Tehillim 92:1-2). Train yourself, as you enjoy the cholent and kishka, the gefilta fish and kugel, to feel that you are eating to celebrate Hashem's creation of the world, affirming your belief that He created the world in six days. You also are rejoicing in the fact that Hashem chose us as His special people.

Use the Shabbos table as a vital platform to impart Torah lessons to your family on a weekly basis. Remember that, although we work the entire week, Shabbos is the acid test of how we would really want to spend our time. So make sure to utilize your holy Shabbos moments—while you are invested with a *neshama y'seirah*, an extra soul—to learn Hashem's Torah and daven more meaningfully. Make sure to eat three meals on Shabbos, for it protects one from the birth pangs of the Messianic times, from the war of Gog and Magog and from the judgments of Gehinnom. Take care to eat a Melave Malka, for besides being an integral part of the process of properly honoring the Shabbos, it is also the way we nurture our *luz* bone. This vital bone is the starting point from which our bodies will be resurrected at the time of *t'chiyas hameisim*—the Resurrection.

The laws of Shabbos are complex and varied. From *borer* to *muktza*, *bishul* to *chazara*, spend time to learn and refresh your knowledge of these vital laws.

13 Elul

Prepare for the Shabbos day—when possible—during the entire week. Shabbos preparation is an extremely lofty occupation. The Gemara teaches us that even Eliyahu HaNavi will not come to herald the arrival of Mashiach on

Friday so as not to disturb our Shabbos preparations. The *Shaarei Teshuva* teaches us that the perspiration generated in preparing for Shabbos is considered as precious to Hashem as tears. Tasting the food before Shabbos in order to ensure its desirability has life-prolonging powers, as the Yerushalmi proves from the words in the Shabbos Mussaf tefillah, "*To'ameha chayim zachu*—One who tastes it, merits life." Rav Yaakov Kamenetsky used to say that in previous generations, Jews faced the challenge of keeping Shabbos. Nowadays, the challenge is how we behave on Erev Shabbos.

14 Elul

The majority of a man's waking hours is spent on earning a living. Be sure to do it with honesty and integrity. After one hundred and twenty years of life, the question, "*Nasasa v'nasata b'emunah*—Did you engage in business with good faith?" will be asked to each of us. Behave every day in a way that you will be able to answer in the affirmative.

Be extremely diligent in paying your employees on time, for laxity in this area can be extremely dangerous. Similarly, the Torah cautions us to make sure to have honest weights and scales in our shops. Treat your workers with fairness and loyalty, always remembering that the way we treat others is the way Hashem will treat us.

15 Elul

The Rosh, in his *Orchos Chaim*, gives one hundred and fifty-six lessons for daily living. The very first piece of advice that he gives is, *"Lehisracheik min hagaivah b'tachlis harichook—* Distance yourself from pride as far as possible." The Rambam says that besides anger, this is the only other trait that one should take an extremist attitude toward and avoid completely. Similarly, in *Pirkei Avos*, the Mishnah (4:4) states in unusually strong terms, *"M'od m'od hevei sh'fal ruach—*Be very, very humble." We are also taught to be *"boreiach min hakavod,"* to flee from honor.

These directives demand from us much personal reflection and introspection, for many of us lead our lives contrary to these admonitions. Since, from a young age, we've been motivated by toys and prizes, rewards and plaques, many of us are still motivated by accolades and praise. In Slabodka, to help knock this way of thinking out of their heads, the *bachurim* would chant the verse, *"To'avas Hashem kol geva leiv—*The haughty are an abomination to Hashem" (Mishlei 16:5), one hundred times.

The huge importance of cultivating humility can be seen from the verse, *"Eikev anava yiras Hashem—*Besides humility, there is the fear of Hashem" (Mishlei 22:4), and Tosfos says (in the twelfth perek of Yevamos) that this pasuk teaches that humility and fear of God are equally important. It is important to note that many feuds and enmities are caused by injured pride. Our Gedolim throughout the generations have always exhibited the trait of humility.

16 Elul

Avoid anger like the plague. Keep in mind the scary Talmudic dictum, *"Kol hakoeis, kol minei Gehinnom sholtin* bo—Those who get angry will need all of the horrific treatments of Gehinnom to repair them" (*Nedarim* 22a). Bear in mind that anger is the fool's way of dealing with problems. As Shlomo Hamelech teaches us, "*Kaas b'cheik k'silim yanuach*—Anger rests in the bosom of a fool" (Koheles 7:9).

No one wants to be friends with an angry person. Even worse, such a person's spouse leads a miserable existence and sees no light at the end of this dismal tunnel. Be especially vigilant not to get angry on Erev Shabbos. Think to yourself that you are only getting upset because the Satan has been given special license to stir up trouble on the anniversary of Adam and Chava's sin on Friday afternoon.

17 Elul

Take health matters very seriously, for the Torah teaches, "*V'nishmartem m'od l'nafshoseichem*—Protect your lives with great care" (Devarim 4:46). This directive forbids the heinous practice of smoking, which is proven to shorten one's life. Get into the habit of wearing seatbelts, have smoke detectors in your home and make sure that your house is childproof—items like window guards and childproof caps on medicines come to mind—if there are children or grandchildren around. The burn units of Cornell and Staten Island Hospitals have a disproportionate amount of religious Jewish patients. This should alert us to the need to exercise great caution with Shabbos candles, Chanukah candles, the *blech*, steaming hot plates of cholent and chicken soup, and any other fire safety situations. Work hard to avoid obesity, which is an epidemic problem in today's society. Keep a look out for other eating disorders in your children, such as anorexia and bulimia. And be wary of alcoholism, which is responsible for breaking up countless marriages and wrecking so many lives.

18 Elul

Make a regular habit of visiting the sick and the elderly (and not just when you feel you have to). The Gemara in *Nedarim* waxes eloquent about the yield of this mitzvah investment more than almost any other mitzvah. It teaches us that visiting the sick saves us from Gehinnom, protects us from suffering, curbs our evil inclination, assures us that people will be honored to associate with us and guarantees us that we'll have good friends.

19 Elul

Cultivate good friends, for they are one of life's greatest treasures. Joy is increased when you have good friends to share it with, and life's sorrows are more manageable when you have friends to help you through them. Stay away from bad friends for, as we learn in *Pirkei Avos* (1:7), they are one of life's greatest dangers—they will drag you with them to doom and destruction.

20 Elul

Give honor to Torah sages and the elderly. (This includes standing up for them.) The reward for this behavior is the rare gift of *yiras Hashem*. Training our children to do likewise also teaches them to respect authority, which will serve them well in all areas of their lives. Parents who act in a cavalier manner with authority in the presence of their children ultimately suffer the most from the consequences of such behavior. Make sure to have a Rav or a Rebbi with whom you consult when you are in doubt. This person will also be there to admonish you when you veer from the correct path. This is a very important insurance to have for a successful life!

21 Elul

Get into the vital habit of reviewing the weekly Torah portion twice along with Rashi/Targum. Everyone looks for a segulah to live long, but this practice is the first life-prolonging device mentioned in Shas. The Chofetz Chaim adds that reviewing the weekly Torah portion helps one acquire *emunah* in Hashem.

22 Elul

Another important step toward longevity is the three-letter word "*Amein*." Learn to say it correctly, taking care not to express it before the bracha is finished. Avoid the reflexive, off-the-cuff *Amein*. Rather, say it meaningfully, knowing before you answer, "I believe," the bracha you are answering to.

The *Chayei Adam* writes that the *Amein* is also a response to the beginning of the bracha, namely "*Boruch Atah Hashem*," and not just to its conclusion, so be sure to focus on the entire bracha. Give special care to the *Amein* answered to the lofty Kaddish prayer. When we say *Amein* to "*Yisgadal v'yiskadash Shemei rabbah* ...," we are affirming our desire to sanctify Hashem, and when we answer *Amein* to "*Oseh shalom bimromav* ..." using the second meaning of *Amein*, namely, "*Kein yehi ratzon*—Let it be Hashem's will," we are fervently asking for peace for ourselves and all of Klal Yisrael.

Answering *Amein* with the proper intent not only prolongs one's life, but it also is the master key to all the gateways of Gan Eden, as the Gemara teaches in *Maseches Shabbos* (119b), "*Kol ha'oneh amein b'chol kocho, poschin lo shaarei Gan Eden*—Whoever answers *Amein* with all his might, all of the gateways of Paradise will be opened for him."

23 Elul

Look for opportunities to make a kiddush Hashem. Drive with consideration. Let someone with just a few items go ahead of you in the store's checkout line. Be courteous in the post office, at the tollbooth and at the bus stop. Be especially vigilant not to cause a chillul Hashem. This includes things like having proper cell phone etiquette, not double-parking and curbing one's temper. Discuss with your children the importance of treating their secular studies teachers with the proper respect. Emphasize that they should use all of the lessons that they learned in their morning *limudei kodesh* when they interact with their English teachers in the afternoon.

Rabbi Moshe Meir Weiss

24 Elul

Never embarrass someone publicly, for it is an easy way to lose your share in the World to Come. Be even more careful with someone's feelings than with someone's money. Pain caused by hurtful words can leave a wound festering for a lifetime.

Judge people favorably. This is a Torah directive—"B'tzedek tishpot amisecha" (Vayikra 19:15). This is especially important to exercise with your spouse. If we judge others favorably, Hashem will judge us favorably. Cultivate this vital trait of seeing the good in others. This talent will enable you to become a chacham, a wise person, as Ben Zoma in Pirkei Avos teaches us: "Who is wise? He who learns from everyone." The only way you can learn from everybody is if you have trained yourself to see the good in each person. This talent will also help you avoid the grave sin of lashon hara, slander, once you've trained yourself to focus on the good and not the bad.

25 Elul

Be forgiving, for Hashem forgives those who are forgiving of others. Get into the habit of forgiving anyone and everyone who wronged you before you go to sleep at night.

26 Elul

Another powerful aid to longevity is to say, "Shema Yisrael Hashem Elokeinu Hashem Echad," with intense concentration, meaningfully appointing Hashem as Master over yourself and declaring that nothing exists independently from Him. Teach yourself to say the Shema lovingly, as we express in our Shabbos Mussaf Kedusha, "*Paamayim b'ahavah Shema omrim*—Twice daily, with love, they say the Shema." Take special care to say it both in the morning and in the evening in its proper time, for the Gemara teaches us that one who says Kriyas Shema in its correct time does an even greater mitzvah than the study of Torah.

27 Elul

Be "*kovaiya itim laTorah*"! Make time without fail for Torah study in every twelve-hour period of your life. Be as regular with this as you are with eating and drinking, for Torah study is the food of the soul. It is the main reason that we were created, as it says in *Pirkei Avos* (2:8), "*Ki l'kach notzarta*—For it is for this (Torah) that you were created." It is the truest happiness in life, as it says, "*Ein simcha k'simchas haTorah*—There is no joy like the joy of Torah," and it is the most beneficial restorative pick-me-up, as it says, "*Toras Hashem temima, m'shivas nafesh*—The Torah of Hashem is perfect, rejuvenating the soul" (Tehillim 19:8). It is a powerful tool for longevity, as it says, "*Ki chaim heim l'motz'eihem*—It is life for those who find them" (Mishlei 4:22). It promises health, as the same pasuk continues, "*Ul'chol b'saro marpei*—And to all his flesh it brings healing." It is the greatest protection against punishment, as we are taught, "*Torah magnei u'matzlei*—The Torah defends and saves," and it is "*k'sris lifnei hapuraniyos*—like a shield before retribution."

Rabbi Moshe Meir Weiss

28 Elul

The Rosh says that tefillin is the most important positive commandment. It, too, has life-prolonging capabilities. As the pasuk says, "*Hashem aleihem yichyu*—Keeping Hashem upon them (by wearing Tefillin) will grant them life" (Yeshaya 38:16). Wear them with thought and meaning to harness the emotions of your heart and the thoughts of your mind to Hashem. Focus on its constant reminder that we should be diligent in our Torah study, as the pasuk says about tefillin, "*Lema'an tihiyeh Toras Hashem beficha*—Wear it in order that the Torah of Hashem should be constantly in your mouths" (Shemos 13:9). Condition yourself that the tefillin should help prevent your head and your heart from harboring thoughts of hate, immorality and lust.

29 Elul

Treasure your tzitzis. The Gemara in *Maseches Shabbos* (32a) teaches us that as a reward for wearing the tzitzis, each of us will merit having 2,800 attendants in the Messianic times. The Sma"k and Rashba"tz both reveal that the Torah directive, "*Ur'isem oso*," to look at the tzitzis, is one of the 613 mitzvos. The Torah teaches us, "*Ur'isem oso uz'chartem es kol mitzvos Hashem*—You should look at the tzitzis and remember all of Hashem's commandments" (Bamidbar 15:39). So train yourself, when seeing your tzitzis, to use them as a vital tool to remind you of your daily responsibilities. They might remind you to give charity or to phone your parents. More profoundly, the tzitzis can remind you to condition yourself to do your good deeds with the thought in mind that you are heeding the commandments of Hashem. As it states, *"Kabeid es avicha v'es imecha ka'asher tziv'cha Hashem Elokecha*—Honor your father and your mother like Hashem commanded you to do" (Shemos 20:12). Don't just honor your parents as a *quid pro quo* for all that they have done for you; rather, keep in mind also that you are fulfilling Hashem's command. Similarly, when you give food to a hungry person, don't just do it because you feel bad for the poor. Do it to fulfill the commandment of Hashem.

One more caveat. In the parsha of tzitzis, the Torah teaches us, *"V'lo sasuru acharei l'vavchem v'acharei eineichem*—You should not turn after your heart and your eyes" (Bamidbar 15:39). Thus, the tzitzis are an aid in our endeavor as a Holy People of *"shmiras ha'einayim,"* guarding our eyes. In today's immodest society, this is a very tall order. Temptations surround us everywhere. However, the *Tuvcha Yabi'u* gives us a powerful incentive. He says that anytime we avoid looking at forbidden things, we create a tremendous *"eis ratzon,"* a time of favor, for ourselves in Hashem's eyes. At the moment we avoid looking at that which is sinful, we can ask Hashem for a boon.

Speaking on this difficult subject, Rav Avigdor Miller teaches that people mistakenly believe that the temptations of the eyes go away by themselves as we get older. He says this is simply not true, and therefore one has to work with great effort to purge oneself of this temptation. The tzitzis can help us strive toward this goal.

1 Tishrei—Rosh Hashanah

Condition yourself to be cognizant of one of the most neglected mitzvah opportunities, namely the mezuzah. Remember that right after the command of the mezuzah, Hashem promises us the great reward, "*Lema'an yirbu y'meichem vimei v'neichem*—In order that you and your children should live long" (Devarim 11:21). So, let's take notice of the mezuzah on each portal that we pass and think for just a second that Hashem is in the room that we are entering and we will try to please Him with whatever we are doing. This discipline can halt many marital disputes and many other mishaps.

2 Tishrei—Rosh Hashanah

Stay far away from feelings of jealousy, for the Rosh says in his *Orchos Chaim* that this is a vicious illness with no cure. So, too, in *Pirkei Avos* (4:21), we are taught that jealousy is one of the three things that can cause a person, *chas v'shalom*, to exit this world early. Keep in mind what we say every morning, "*She'asa li kol tzarki*," that Hashem has given you everything you need to be happy.

3 Tishrei—Tzom Gedalyah

With all your might, keep your distance from any kind of fighting. "*Machlokes*" is an anagram of the words "*cheilek maves*," a portion of death. Rav Avigdor Miller teaches us that when the ground opened up to swallow Korach, it was not an isolated event. Rather, it is a model for all of us to learn from. Indeed, many people are swallowed up in an early grave because they got involved in fighting and feuds. One of the best gifts you can give your children is to tell them at a very young age that your family is allergic to fighting like others are allergic to penicillin and bee bites. Plead with them that throughout their lives they should avoid getting mixed up in any sort of quarrel, whether in shul, in school, in the workplace, at the club or in the bungalow colony.

In his ethical will, Rav Shamshon Raphael Hirsch asked his children for just one thing—that they should preserve peace between each other!

Pursue peace at all costs for, as Rashi says in Parshas Bechukosai, it is, *"shakul k'neged hakol*—equal to everything else."* As we say in our morning liturgy, *"Oseh shalom u'vorei es hakol*—Hashem makes peace and creates everything else."* To achieve peace, it is worth giving up much and looking away plenty, for the alternative is the ruination of life. As Rashi also says, *"Im ein shalom, ein klum*—Without peace there is nothing."* The importance of this pursuit cannot be emphasized sufficiently. The Rambam says at the end of Hilchos Chanuka, *"Shekol haTorah kula nitan la'asos shalom b'olam, shene'emar, 'Deracheha darchei noam, v'chol nesivoseha shalom'*—The entire Torah was given to ensure peace in the world, as it states, 'Its ways are ways of sweetness and all its paths are paths of peace.'"* It is impossible to be a true Ben Torah or Bas Yisrael without embracing the pursuit of shalom.

4 Tishrei

Master the trait of silence, for it will save you much aggravation and distress. As it states in *Sanhedrin* (7a), *"Tovei d'shama v'adish; cholfei bishtei mei'a*—Fortunate is one who hears and doesn't answer; one hundred bad times will pass him by." The supreme importance of this trait can be seen from the famous dictum in *Pirkei Avos* (1:17) where Rebbi Shimon teaches us, *"Kol yamai gadalti bein hachachamim, v'lo matzasi l'guf tov mishtika*—All of my days I grew up amongst the Sages and I didn't find anything better for the body than knowing how to keep silent." The Gemara also teaches us in *Maseches Chullin* (89a), *"Mah umnaso shel adam b'olam hazeh? Yaaseh atzmo k'ileim*—What should be a person's profession be in this world? He should know how to make himself like a mute."

5 Tishrei

Be first to greet people and do so with a smile. As we are taught in *Pirkei Avos* (1:15), *"Hevei m'kabel kol adam b'seiver panim yafos*—Greet all people with a smiling countenance." Remember the sage advice of Ben Zoma, *"Aizehu mechubad? Hamechabeid es habriyos*—Who is respected? He who honors others" (*Pirkei Avos* 4:1). Wish people well, for the Torah guarantees, *"Va'avar'cha m'var'checha*—I will bless those who bless you" (Bereishis 12:3).

6 Tishrei

Learn how to compliment others genuinely. You will become loved, because everyone treasures a compliment. It is an inexpensive way to spread good cheer and bring out the best in people. There are many vehicles to use to express these compliments—in person, on the phone, in a letter, via email. Utilize them all. Exercise this art, especially with your spouse and with your children.

Use criticism sparingly, especially in the home. Constant criticism is one of the most frequent roads to an unhappy environment. Bear in mind that criticism comes naturally when we feel something is wrong or lacking, but compliments are not an automatic response. Rather, we must train ourselves to express them, knowing that they are a wonderful lubricant for all of our relationships.

7 Tishrei

The *Yerushalmi* in *Peah* relates a frightening teaching: Just as Torah is considered the greatest mitzvah, so is *lashon hara* considered the worst sin. Even if what a person says is true and relating it gives him much relief from his distress, sharing bad information about someone with another person—except in rare cases—is a grievous sin. The Torah cautions us, "*Arur makeh rei'eihu baseiser*—Cursed is he who smites his friend in secret," and the *Targum Yonasan* says that this refers to one who speaks *lashon hara*.

This is, very literally, a matter of life and death for, as we are taught, "*Hamaves v'hachaim b'yad halashon*—Death and life are in the hands of the tongue," and as the saintly Chofetz Chaim taught us, "*Mi ha'ish hechafetz chaim, oheiv yomim, liros tov? N'tzor l'shoncha meira*—Who is the man who desires life, who loves days, to see good? Let him guard his tongue from speaking evil."

This is the only mitzvah that we ask Hashem to help us with in our daily prayers, as we beseech Him, "*Elokai, n'tzor lishoni mei'ra*—My God, guard my tongue from speaking evil." The Gemara in *Sanhedrin* shares with us an amazing fundamental of life. "*Adam la'amal peh nivra*—A person's greatest arena for achievement in life is with his mouth." Thus, the challenge of avoiding *lashon hara* is one of the greatest accomplishments that a human being can achieve in this world. The Vilna Gaon declares that for every word of *lashon hara* that we avoid saying, we are rewarded with the *ohr haganuz*, the hidden light in the Afterlife.

8 Tishrei

Do not tell a lie. The Torah does not simply say, "*Lo s'shakru*—Thou shall not lie." Rather, it cautions us even more severely, "*Mid'var sheker tirchak*—Distance yourself from a false word." This is a very difficult task, for many of us fib our way out of sticky predicaments all the time. Others have the bad habit of altering the truth to build themselves up or to be the life of the party. We must know, however, that veering from the truth is an extremely severe crime—so much so that the Gemara teaches us that one who does so habitually will not be granted entry in the "*mechitza*," the partition of Hashem in the World to Come.

9 Tishrei

One of the very best defenses in life is giving tzedaka, as the Gemara in *Baba Basra* says, "*Tzedaka tatzil mimaves*— Charity saves one from death." The reason that charity has more of a life-giving quality than other mitzvos can be explained mathematically. If a person makes $25 an hour, and he gives $100 to a poor person, he is essentially giving away four hours of his life. We are taught that Hashem rewards at a ratio of 500 to 1. Thus, a tzedaka investment of four hours would yield a person 2,000 hours of life.

Tzedaka is also one of the very best financial investments, as the Torah guarantees us, "*Aser t'aser*—You shall surely tithe," which the Gemara explains to mean, "*Aser bishvil shetisasher*—Give tithes in order to become wealthy." Furthermore, tzedaka promises us tranquility, as it teaches in *Pirkei Avos*, "*Marbeh tzedaka, marbeh shalom*—One who increases his charity output will increase his harmony."

Included in our tzedaka efforts are the many different forms of chesed. Remember, this is the very lifeblood of the Jewish people who are by nature *rachmanim* and *gomlei chasadim*, people of compassion and doers of loving-kindness. Make sure to have a regular dosage of *hachnassas kallah*, helping the indigent groom and bride, *levayas hameis*, giving proper respect to the dead, and *v'hechezacta bo*, strengthening a fellow Jew in need. In today's day and age, there is a vital need to help people find their shidduch, their life's mate, and to help the many people who are out of work find employment. Finally, whatever we can do to help strengthen people's marriages, especially our own, is a huge mitzvah in the eyes of our Creator.

10 Tishrei—Yom Kippur

Combat your natural inclination to be selfish. Remember, we are urged, "*V'halachta bidrachav*—Walk in the ways of Hashem." Hashem can only be a Giver because there is nothing for Him to take—He is the "*Konei HaKol*, the Owner of Everything." Therefore, if we want to emulate Hashem, we need to become givers as well. This is the very essence of life in this world, as we are taught, "*Olam chesed yibaneh*—This world is built upon kindness."

This is the first reason that the Torah gives for the institution of marriage, as it says, "*Lo tov heyos he'adam l'vado*—It is not good for man to be alone," for when he is alone, he caters only to himself and wallows in his self-centeredness. The way we raise ourselves above the animal level is to train ourselves to do selflessly for others. In that way, we make ourselves different from the animals, which know only about self-gratification. We should try every day to do at least one thing that is wholly selfless, dedicated solely to the benefit of another.

Rabbi Moshe Meir Weiss

The Elul Spirit

The Elul Spirit

It's hard to believe, but it's that time of the year again. The month of Elul is upon us.

As we try to enjoy those last precious moments of our summer vacations, our minds are already busy with thoughts of school supplies lists and new bus routes. Summer wanes and our thoughts start to focus on getting back into the yearly grind.

Of course, to an observant Jew, the month of Elul means so much more than school lists and bus routes. We are taught, "*Hakol holeich achar hachesom*—Everything goes according to the finale." Thus, this month, the last month of the Jewish year, is the decisive one when it comes to determining how successful our year has been. In the same way that one can correct the deeds of an entire life on one's last day, so, too, one can greatly improve the previous year in this final, crucial month.

We are taught that Moshe Rabbeinu went up Har Sinai to appeal for forgiveness over the sin of the Golden Calf on the first day of Elul, and, after staying there for forty days and forty nights, he came down on Yom Kippur having achieved atonement for Klal Yisrael. Moshe Rabbeinu thus injected into this time of year a powerful opportunity for one to repent and mend one's ways. That is why this time of the year is known as the Y'mei Rachamim v'Selicha (days of mercy and forgiveness).

The *Chayei Adam* writes in Chapter 138 of his sefer that it is incumbent upon a God-fearing Jew to prepare at least thirty days before Rosh Hashanah to be ready for the Day of Judgment. Moreover, the Alter of Kelm relates that it is absurd to say the verses of *Malchiyos* (Kingship), and to realistically accept Hashem as our King in the Rosh Hashanah davening, without having amply prepared beforehand. He makes the following frightening statement: To recite *Malchiyos* on Rosh Hashanah in an "off the cuff" manner is even worse than saying Viduy (confession) on Rosh Hashanah! Saying Viduy on Rosh Hashanah is a practice from which we abstain, since it would be wrong to confess openly during the moments when we are being judged. Yet, according to the *Chayei Adam*, reciting *Malchiyos* without the proper preparation would be worse.

So how do we prepare? What are we supposed to do to ready ourselves? Of course, the answer is to do teshuvah. But what exactly is "teshuvah"? The meaning of this word is not as simple as it sounds. The word teshuvah has two meanings that seem to contradict one another. This can be illustrated by the following two verses. In the verse, "*Vayashav Avraham el n'arav*—And Avraham returned to his young men" (Bereishis 22:19), teshuvah means to return. In the verse, "*Shuv meicharon apecha*—Forsake Your anger" (Shemos 32:12), teshuvah means to abandon or to forsake.

The Rambam explains that the word teshuvah should be translated in the latter sense, interpreting it as the process of abandoning and forsaking our sins. However, both the Maharal of Prague and the Mabit explain that teshuvah has more to do with return. Teshuvah describes man's attempt to return to Hashem.

Let us focus on this latter interpretation. Indeed, the job of returning to Hashem is the focus of the verse, "*V'shavta ad Hashem Elokecha*—And you will return to Hashem your God" (Devarim 30:2). We were given a positive command: "*Es Hashem Elokecha Tirah*—You shall fear Hashem your God" (Devarim 6:13). How do we fulfill this command on a practical basis? Does this mitzvah expect us to tremble at the thought of the Almighty? The Rishonim teach us that if we are tempted to, for instance, speak *lashon hara*, berate our spouse or gaze at improper things, and we abstain, it is because we realize that Hashem is watching us. This is the very essence of "*Es Hashem Elokecha Tirah.*" We know that Hashem is always present and we are afraid of doing wrong before Him. This is how we fulfill the commandment of fearing God. This mindset is consistent with the deeper focus of Elul—being more aware that Hashem is around.

In Elul, we sense Hashem's presence.

However, Hashem should not be thought of only as an inhibiting factor. Hashem should also be our primary motivation for doing well. The pasuk teaches us, "*B'chol d'rachecha da'eihu*—In all your ways you should acknowledge Him" (Mishlei 3:6). We debate within ourselves: Should I get up early for Selichos or sleep another tempting half-an-hour? Should I travel an entire hour to visit a sick person or browse the latest sports page? When we decide to do the mitzvah because we want to please Hashem, this is a true embodiment of *yiras Shamayim.*

In our Yamim Noraim liturgy, we say, "*Teshuvah,*

tefillah, u'tzedaka ma'avirin es ro'ah hagezeirah—Repentance, prayer and charity abolish the evil of the decree." Prayer is a very important item to work on at this time of year. Working on our davening is consistent with the theme of returning to Hashem. In order to pray properly and succeed in our prayers, we must realize that everything depends upon Hashem. When praying, we must feel as if we are talking to Hashem and we must believe with certainty that our davening is important, and that it will really help. Many people think that working on davening means to learn the meaning of the words and to concentrate on them. This is important, but it is not the first step. Rather, we must first learn to realize that when we pray, we are talking to God. Once we allow this realization to shape our davening, everything else will just come naturally.

Let us remember that in direct proportion to how much we feel *"Ani l'Dodi*—I am to my Beloved (Hashem)," that is how much *"v'Dodi li"*—my Beloved will pay attention to me. So let's make an effort to think of Hashem frequently. When we pass a mezuzah, as we do countless times each day, let's take a moment and think about how Hashem is in the room with us. Let us think, "Thank you, God," every time we say a blessing. Let us make it a firm practice to start off our day with a meaningful "thank you" in Modeh Ani. Let's try to end our day with heartfelt gratitude as expressed in the bracha of Hamapil.

If we pepper our days throughout the month of Elul with constant acknowledgments of Hashem, we will then truly be ready this Rosh Hashanah to coronate Hashem as our King.

What's on Your Mind?

Every day, at the end of Shemoneh Esrei, we part from Hashem with the request, "*Yehi ratzon mil'fanecha, Hashem Elokeinu vEilokei avoseinu, sheyibaneh Beis Hamikdash bimheira v'yameinu*—May it be Your will, Hashem, that You rebuild the Temple speedily in our days." Our desire to have the Beis Hamikdash stems from the fact that we want Hashem to reside in our midst. When we had the Temple, the pasuk testifies, "*V'asu li Mikdash v'shachanti b'socham*—Make for Me a sanctuary that I may dwell amongst you" (Shemos 25:8).

However, according to Rav Avigdor Miller, *zt"l*, the real purpose of the Temple is to train us to develop our minds into a sanctuary, meaning that Hashem should always reside in our thoughts. This is how Rav Miller explains the Gemara in *Maseches Brachos* (33) that states, "*Kol mi she'yesh lo dei'a, k'ilu nivneh Beis Hamikdash b'yamav*—Whoever has knowledge, it is as if the Temple is built in his day." What is the connection between personal knowledge and the Holy Temple? The answer is that "*dei'a*" refers to the true knowledge of awareness of Hashem, as the verse states, "*Hein *yiras Hashem hi chachma*—Behold the awareness of Hashem is wisdom" (Iyov 28:28). So, too, Tehillim (111:10) teaches us, "*Reishis chachma yiras Hashem*—The beginning of wisdom is awareness of Hashem" (because the word "*yirah*" can mean "to see, to be aware"). Thus, a person who has an awareness of Hashem has made himself a veritable Temple, where God constantly resides.

> When we strive to maintain an awareness of Hashem's Presence in our lives, we make ourselves into veritable Temples.

This idea sheds light on another famous Talmudic dictum, "*Shekulah misasan shel tzaddikim kisreifas Beis Elokeinu*—The death of the righteous is equivalent to the burning of the Temple" (*Rosh Hashanah* 18b). The righteous person—here defined as one who lives with Hashem constantly in his thoughts—is analogous to the Temple, and thus his death is synonymous with its destruction.

This is the meaning of *kedusha*, holiness. Before we make a bracha, we often voice the sentiment, "*Asher kid'shanu b'mitzvosav*—Who sanctified us (made us holy) with His commandments." What is the nature of this holiness? It is a heightened awareness of Hashem—that very awareness that brachos are meant to engender in us. When we do something because God commanded us to do so, it makes us more aware of Hashem in our lives.

We pray for this awareness in our very first request every day in the Shemoneh Esrei, "*Atah chonein l'adam da'as*—you grant a person knowledge." So, it is no coincidence that this bracha follows right on the heels of the blessing of holiness, "*HaKeil HaKadosh*," because when a person achieves this awareness, he has achieved a level of holiness, which is the main pursuit of life. As Moshe Rabbeinu himself said, "*Mah Hashem Elokecha sho'eil me'imach ki im l'yirah es Hashem Elokecha*—What does Hashem your God ask from you but that you should be aware of Him?*" (Devarim 10:12).

Consider that the word "*chaim*," which means life, is composed of two words, "*moach*" (brain) and "*Yud Yud*" (representing Hashem), which indicates that this goal of constantly striving for an awareness of Hashem is the essence of life. Furthermore, the gematria of the word "*chaim*" is 68, which has the same numerical value as the word "*chacham*," a wise person, for true wisdom means to be aware of Hashem at all times.

In a similar vein, when a chassan tells his kallah under the chuppah, "*Harei at m'kudeshes li*—You are hereby sanctified to me," he is expressing the sentiment that he will keep her in his mind always. As previously mentioned, Rav Yaakov Kamenetsky, *zt"l*, would always advise brides and grooms that from the moment of the chuppah onwards they should cease to think in terms of "I." Their focus should always be in terms of "we."

Hashem has given us a body of laws known as *eidos*, testimonials, to aid us in keeping Him in our thoughts. For example, the mezuzah confronts us upon entering every room and as we head off to engage in our business, to remind us that Hashem is watching us in whatever we do. Likewise, the tefillin on our arms and heads is meant to stir us to keep Hashem in our hearts and in our minds. The tzitzis are to remind us that we are members of Hashem's hosts, clothed in army uniform, and the yarmulke, which is derived from the words "*Yarei Malka*—to be aware of the King," is meant to help us develop this all-important wisdom.

When we live with awareness of Hashem, not only are we fulfilling the purpose of the world, as it states in the Sheva Brachos, "*Shehakol bara lichvodo*—Everything was created for His honor," but it also helps to prevent us from sinning. If that isn't enough, striving for this awareness of Hashem promises us longevity, as it states, "*Yiras Hashem tosif yamim*—Awareness of Hashem adds length to one's days" (Mishlei 10:27). During the Yamim Noraim, when Hashem's Presence is felt more intensely and awareness of Hashem is so important, may we be *zocheh* to develop this discipline and transform ourselves into mini-Sanctuaries.

It's Never Too Late

One of the most lethal and dangerous weapons that the Yetzer Hara uses to catch us is to get us to give up and feel that all is lost and that there is no return. Once we feel defeated, the Yetzer Hara has us in the palm of his hand—right where he wants us to be!

It is human nature to start to feel beaten or overwhelmed. If a person has committed numerous sins, he begins to believe that he can never make up for them. He harbors feelings of worthlessness and feels he is sinking into a hole. That's when the Yetzer Hara has won the battle. If we study Chazal, we see important, encouraging lessons about many great people who lived in great distress, yet succeeded in pulling themselves up out of the depths of despair. Indeed, in the times of darkest gloom, the *yeshua* could be right around the corner. And what a wondrous salvation it could be!

The Gemara in *Brachos* (10a) gives us an example. The Navi Yeshaya came to Chizkiya and told him: *"Ki mais atah, v'lo sichyeh*—You will die and you will not live" (Melachim Beis 20:1). Why the redundancy of words? The Gemara explains that the Navi was telling Chizkiya that he would not only die now in Olam Hazeh, but also that he would not receive his share in Olam Habah. What worse news is it possible for a Jew to hear? Not only was his life forfeited, but his eternity as well!

Receiving devastating news often sends a person into deep despair—so much so that he can break down completely. However, the Gemara continues its narrative and tells us that Chizkiya told the Navi to finish his prophecy and leave. And then what did he do? Chizkiya davened to Hashem. He poured out his heart. He evoked the *zechus Avos*, the merits of the Forefathers. He reminded Hashem of meritorious acts he had done in the past. When he had finished, he was saved. Hashem accepted his davening and his teshuvah. When a person is faced with horrible news, the worst imaginable, he cannot let himself give up. That's what the Yetzer Hara wants.

> When faced with terrible challenges, we cannot give up. That's just what the Yetzer Hara wants.

The Gemara in *Gittin* that we learn on Tisha B'Av tells us about a horrible man, the mass murderer Nevuzaradan, who killed 94,000 Jews on one rock. He was a bloodthirsty killer who slaughtered almost one million Jews. Not many people are worse than that. Yet, he went on to become a *ger tzedek*, a righteous convert. None of us has committed such terrible deeds as Nevuzaradan. We should learn from this that if a person like Nevuzaradan can turn himself around after the wicked things he did, then it is certainly possible for us to mend our ways. It is never too late.

Let's look at another example of someone who never gave up. Rabbi Akiva started to learn the Aleph Bais when he was forty years old, and he became one of the greatest leaders and teachers of Klal Yisrael. From Rabbi Akiva we learn that we

Rabbi Moshe Meir Weiss

have to use our time wisely. We don't know what successes might be waiting for us in the future. Rabbi Akiva learned and taught and cultivated 24,000 talmidim. Imagine, if you will, the Siyum Daf Yomi in Madison Square Garden. Imagine having enough talmidim to fill Madison Square Garden! Rabbi Akiva devoted himself to teaching these students and making them into Gedolei Yisrael. And what happened? Every last one of them contracted diphtheria and died. Rabbi Akiva lost his life's work in one blow. However, Rabbi Akiva did not throw up his hands and give up. He went out again and started from scratch. He did not look back. He forged ahead and returned with a select handful of talmidim who were so great that they carried the torch of Torah into the next generation and for generations to come.

Another great person who we can learn from was Yocheved. Yocheved was the mother of what was perhaps the greatest family in all of history. She was the mother of the man who brought us the Torah and spoke to Hashem *"panim el panim*—face to face." Her older son was the first Kohen Gadol. She was the mother of the spokeswoman of the Jewish women at Kriyas Yam Suf and in whose merit B'nei Yisrael were given water in the desert for forty years. Yet, for most of her life, Yocheved was childless. She did not give birth to Miriam until she was 124 years old. She saw her friends and peers, and those much younger than herself, having children. Yet Yocheved did not despair. She did not withdraw within herself but—just the opposite— busied herself in caring for children. She became a midwife so that in that merit she would be worthy to have her own children. Because the *m'yaldos*, the midwives, feared Hashem more than they did Pharaoh, and they saved the Jewish children, they were rewarded. *"Va'yaas lahem batim*—They had dynasties."

Let's take a look at another example. In *Megillas Rus*, we are told about a man named Boaz. The name Boaz is derived from two words: *"bo az"*—here there is strength. The *Me'am Loez* tells us that the name Boaz contains the same letters as the word *"azav"*—to leave, to forsake. Boaz forsook the Yetzer Hara. He had great fortitude. The Gemara in *Baba Basra* (91a) tells us that Boaz had a far from easy life. He had sixty children: thirty sons and thirty daughters. He buried every one of them, and his wife as well. A tragedy so great could cause anyone to go over the edge. However, Boaz did not give up. He married Rus and had another child.

The Megillah tells us, *"Va'teiled bein*—And she bore a son."* Why doesn't it say, *"Va'teiled lo bein*—And she bore *to him* a son"? Rav Alkovitz, in the sefer *K'tzir Chitim*, explains that on the very night the baby was conceived, Boaz died. The people of that time said that this was a punishment because he married a Moavite woman. But history proves that he was supposed to marry Rus and conceive a child. As we know, that child was Oved, who in turn had Yishai, who in turn had Dovid. This was the beginning of Malchus Beis Dovid and the Melech HaMashiach. Shmuel HaNavi wrote *Megillas Rus* in order to publicize the fact that it was definitely in accordance with Halacha for Rus to convert (*"Moavi v'lo Moavis"*) and that Boaz's p'sak was correct. We should never be tested in the terrible ways that Boaz was. However, we have to realize that life can throw us a few curves, and if they come our way, we should take heart.

The situation might not seem good, but we never know what good might be in store.

In the first perek of *Pirkei Avos*, the Mishnah tells us: "*Al tisyaeish min hapuraniyus.*" The Machzor Vitri offers an explanation of this statement that fits in with our theme: Do not give up hope because you are expecting retribution. For example, a person may not be careful enough in his kashrus, may be harsh toward his spouse or children or lack devotion in his davening and so on. Because of these sins, he knows that he deserves punishment. He knows it is coming. So he tells himself that he is a lost soul and that's that! Instead of feeling hopeless and lost, he should remember that Hashem does not want him to be punished. "*Ki lo yachpotz b'mos hameis*—For Hashem does not desire the death of the wicked." Hashem wants him to do teshuvah—"*ki im b'shuvo midarko v'chaya*—but rather that he turn away from his evil path, and then he will live." So don't despair over what you may have done. It's past history.

In *Pirkei Avos* (4:11), it says that repentance and good deeds are like a shield against punishment ("*kisris bifnei hapuraniyus*"). These two vital ingredients work together and protect us from retribution.

Our first piece of armor is teshuvah, repentance. Start by correcting the *chisaron*, the lack—be ashamed of the act you've committed. The Gemara in *Brachos* teaches us that *busha* (shame) is a good middah to have. In fact, if someone is ashamed of a sin he's committed, Hashem forgives him for all of his sins. *Busha* is a positive feeling. It leads to good.

"*Yi'ush*" (despair), on the other hand, is negative and nothing good will come of it. We see how useless, even destructive, *yi'ush* can be when we compare the lives of Rus and Orpah. Rus and Orpah both expressed a desire to stay with Naomi and convert to Judaism. Naomi tried to dissuade them. Finally, Orpah turned aside and went back to Moav. She felt such despair and sadness that she just gave up, and that very night she became a harlot. Rus did not despair. She followed Naomi, suffered poverty and shame and eventually merited becoming the mother of the Davidic dynasty.

All the examples we've discussed should strengthen us and teach us that we should never give up. We can always change the situation. We can turn ourselves around. Let us take *chizuk* from all the examples we've studied—from Rabbi Akiva, Yocheved, Boaz, Chizkiya and even Nevuzaradan. The next time we feel like giving up, let's remember all these great people who never despaired. May we all be *zocheh* to succeed in doing teshuvah properly and not fall into the hands of despair. May we always be full of hope, and may Hashem fulfill all our requests for good and bless us with good health so that we may serve Him to the best of our capabilities and potential.

Changing for the Better

Doing teshuvah is a complex task. One of the meanings of the word "teshuvah" is to repent or abandon sin. But we need to work on purging our faults and imperfections in order to abandon our sins.

We all realize that facing our own imperfections is no easy task. The Gemara tells us that we have a natural inclination to ignore our own faults. "*Ein adam roeh nigei atzmo*—One does not see his own blemishes." We can always easily spot a sour co-worker's greed, our relative's stinginess or our neighbor's arrogance. However, when it comes to our own vices, we seem to have a blind spot. Seeing through this blind spot is the difficult task that confronts us every Elul when we are challenged to take a brutal and blunt look at ourselves. Nevertheless, it's time to face the music.

Self-analysis, the pursuit of our real selves, is called making a Cheshbon Hanefesh. A practical way to go about this is to scrutinize what we do from the moment we awake until the time we go to sleep. We should consider the "small" things—how we smile at our loved ones in the morning and whether we are forgiving of others' deeds before retiring. We should notice how we wash our hands upon awakening, and the care we give to Kriyas Shema al Hamitah before our slumber. All these and many other daily activities merit careful analysis.

"Wait!" you might exclaim. "I didn't go through this arduous process last year and I seemed to have a pretty good year anyway. So I'll probably have the same type of fortune this coming year. Maybe I'm even a little better this year than last." This is faulty reasoning. The Mishnah in *Pirkei Avos* (1:7) teaches us, "*Al tisyaeish min hapuraniyus*—Don't despair from retribution." We never know what sins are building up in our account and when, *chas v'shalom*, the final straw may break the camel's back. Let's not let the Yetzer Hara lull us into a false sense of security.

If we manage to stay away from false complacency, the Yetzer Hara will try a different tactic. "Why should I bother with all these commitments and protestations of regret when experience has shown that they only last through the Days of Awe? Year after year, I promise to pray more sincerely, speak more gently and all sorts of other things, and by the time winter comes, I'm invariably back to my old tricks. So why all the effort? Who do think I'm really fooling?"

Can't you hear the voice of the Yetzer Hara in this convincing argument? Can't you just hear him pleading and cajoling you to do anything but occupy yourself with spiritual improvement?

I believe that in answer to these murmurings the Midrash teaches us, "'*V'atah pen yishlach yado* … — And now, lest he extend his hand [to take from the Tree of Life].' *Ein 'v'atah' ela lashon teshuvah*—the term 'and now' refers to repentance" (Bereishis Rabbah 21:6). The standard explanation of this Midrash is that we should not fall into the

We should never put off doing teshuvah.

trap of procrastinating repentance. We shouldn't push off teshuvah by reasoning that we'll learn when we retire or that we'll spend time with the children when they mature, and so on. Rather, we should concentrate on sincere repentance *now*. Therefore, "and now" refers to teshuvah.

Once we've ferreted out our sins and imperfections, teshuvah consists of a four-step program. These steps are regret and contrition, abandoning the sin, verbal confession and a firm commitment to avoid sinning in the future.

The first step, regret and contrition, harnesses a very powerful emotion. In *Maseches Brachos* (12b), Rav teaches us that whoever feels shame over a sin that he transgressed achieves forgiveness for that sin. This is a rather special bonanza. Often, after making a spiritual accounting, we feel guilt-ridden and depressed and see ourselves full of ugly blemishes. If, however, we feel an honest sense of shame over how we've been yelling at our spouse, neglecting our parents or talking absent-mindedly to God, for instance, our shame can be a potent step in the direction of spiritual purification and betterment.

The Midrash offers an example of how it is proper to feel bad over our misdeeds, and the extent to which our feelings of remorse can be taken. The Midrash reminds us of a man named Ohn ben Peles. Ohn ben Peles participated in Korach's rebellion against Moshe Rabbeinu. The Midrash relates that the name Ohn has as its root the word *"onein"* (to grieve). This is because Ohn ben Peles spent the rest of his life grieving and regretting his willingness to be a part of the wicked assembly of Korach.

In the first chapter of Hilchos Teshuvah, the Rambam

gives us the following formula to use when we want to verbally confess a specific sin: *"Ana, Hashem, chatasi, avisi, pashati l'fanecha b'avon hachamur shel* _____, (e.g., *lashon hara*), *v'harai ani nichamti uvoshti b'maasai ul'olam eini chozeir l'davar zeh*—Please Hashem, I have sinned, transgressed and rebelled before you with the severe sin of _____, (e.g., *lashon hara*), and I am grieved and embarrassed by my actions, and I will never return to this practice."

When it comes to future commitments, we should know that Hashem does not expect an immediate and total turnaround. *"Ki lo yachpotz b'mos hameis, ki im b'shuvo midarko v'chaya."* Hashem doesn't want to see anyone die. It's a change of direction that's the important thing. Hashem is patient with us as we strive for progress on our road to recovery.

We certainly have our work cut out for us. Let's start making those personal accountings and try to improve ourselves both in the arena of *"bein adam l'chaveiro*—between ourselves and our fellow man," and *"bein adam l'Makom*—between ourselves and Hashem." In this merit. may we find favor in Hashem's eyes and have His assistance as we try to truly mend our ways.

Time and Klal Yisrael

The concept of time is of utmost importance to Klal Yisrael. Rav Soloveitchik explains that we see how important the concept of time is from the very first mitzvah that Hashem commanded B'nei Yisrael. Right after Makas Bechoros, Hashem gave B'nei Yisrael their first commandment as a nation: "*Hachodesh hazeh lachem rosh chadashim*—This month (Nissan) will be the first month for you" (Shemos 12:2). The very first mitzvah we received as a nation was the mitzvah of Rosh Chodesh.

The command to start keeping time points to the transformation B'nei Yisrael was undergoing. A slave has no concept of time. Each day is just like the day before. There is no difference from one day to the next, from one week to the next, from one month to the next. B'nei Yisrael was suffering from *avodas perech*—non-stop, backbreaking labor. The men never came home. They spent twenty-four hours a day laboring out in the fields, working and sleeping. Time was just one long period of drudgery, never changing, always the same. However, when B'nei Yisrael became a nation, Hashem gave them the mitzvah of time. For the Jewish nation, days and times became unique and distinctive.

In our Shabbos davening, we say, "*Limnos yameinu kein hoda v'navi l'vav chachma*" (Tehillim 90:12). Literally translated, this means that if we count our days, it will bring us to the heart of wisdom. Anyone can count his days; even the most simple-minded person knows how old he is. But if a person counts the days he has *remaining* instead of the days of his life that have passed, he will come to the heart of wisdom. If a person realizes how limited his days are, then he will reach a deep understanding.

> If we focus on the time remaining to us instead of the days that we have lived, we will attain wisdom.

There is a deeper meaning of this tefillah as well. The word "*limnos*" has another translation. It is derived from the verb meaning "to appoint." A person has to "appoint" his days—to act in accordance with the time of year. During the year, there are appropriate times for mourning the Beis Hamikdash, for being happy, for *zerizus* in Torah and for working on our relationships with others. We say in davening, "*Mekadeish Yisrael v'haz'manim*—Hashem sanctified Yisrael and the times." We understand this to mean that Hashem sanctified Yisrael, who in turn sanctified the times by declaring Rosh Chodesh.

We have come now to a critical period in our year—the month of Elul has arrived. The Rosh HaYeshiva in Novardok would give a loud clap on the table and announce, "Only 33 days to Elul." That would be enough for the talmidim to get the message and return to their studies with new vigor. The Arizal, based on the Zohar Hakadosh, explains the pasuk,

"*U'vachsa es aviha v'es ima yerech yamim*—And she will cry for her father and her mother thirty days" (Devarim 21:13), that the thirty days being discussed refer to the month of Elul. When you extend the thirty days of Elul into the first ten days of Tishrei, you arrive at an important total of forty days. The first letters of the pasuk, "*Ani l'Dodi v'Dodi li*," stand for the month of Elul. The last letter in each word is a Yud. Four Yuds equal forty—the forty days from Rosh Chodesh Elul to Yom Kippur. The Shelah Hakadosh tells us how important it is that we start counting the time from the first day of Rosh Chodesh Elul so that we have forty complete days to Yom Kippur—forty days to do teshuvah.

Why are these forty days designated as the time for teshuvah? On the 17th of Tammuz, Moshe Rabbeinu came down from Har Sinai, saw the B'nei Yisrael sinning with the Golden Calf and broke the luchos. Forty days later, on Yom Kippur, he descended with the new and enduring luchos. The forty days from Rosh Chodesh Elul to Yom Kippur were a time of fasting and repentance. Moshe Rabbeinu begged Hashem for forgiveness and earned our salvation. This time is fixed for eternity as a time for repentance. "*Mishenichnas Elul marbin b'teshuvah*—When Elul comes in, we emphasize teshuvah." For all generations, this is the time of year that is reserved for atonement.

It is brought down in the *Tzetel Katan* that if someone wishes to adopt a good custom, and he observes that custom for forty consecutive days, it will become second nature to him. Why forty days? Why not something to do with the number three, which represents *chazaka*, establishing something as fact in Halacha? Chazal explain to us that it takes forty days for the creation of the embryo in the mother's womb. After the first forty days of pregnancy, it is futile, even forbidden, to pray that the child should be either a boy or a girl. At that point, the embryo is formed and praying for either a boy or girl would be useless.

To create a new being, to change an ingrained nature and recreate yourself, takes forty days. In the forty days between Elul and Yom Kippur, we must break our bad habits. We must create a new *teva*, a new nature within ourselves. Moshe Rabbeinu needed to be on Har Sinai for forty days to absorb and understand all of the Torah. The Mabul, which wiped out the existing world and heralded the rebirth of the universe, lasted forty days. We need these precious forty days in which to change ourselves. Let's not procrastinate! We tend to think that the Aseres Y'mei Teshuvah are when we really have to work at it. But it's not so! In order to really change ourselves, we need all the time given us.

The name Elul is the Babylonian name for the month. Why should we use a Babylonian name for such an important and holy month? In the parsha of the Meraglim, the Targum explains the phrase, "*v'yasuru es ha'aretz—*and you should scout out the land," (Bamidbar 13:2) and translates it as "*v'yisalelum yas ara'ah.*" The word "*v'yisalelum*" has the same root as the word Elul. Elul is the Aramaic word that means to scout. That is the job of Elul. We must scout out our actions and deeds. One of the greatest problems at this time of the year is that the Yetzer Hara tells us to put off doing teshuvah. But we must act now, before the deadline. Our version of April 15th is approaching fast and we must pay our dues.

The Alter of Kelm tells us of a seeming contradiction in what the *Shulchan Aruch* tells us to do on Erev Rosh Hashanah. In one paragraph, we are told that Erev Yom Tov is a time for preparation. One should bathe and get a haircut on Erev Rosh Hashanah so that there is a feeling of simcha as we approach the Yom HaDin. In another paragraph, however, we are told that the *Mishnah Berurah* brings down a minhag to fast a half a day on Erev Rosh Hashanah from the fear of the judgment. The Alter explains this contradiction. A person should act happy because of the *zechus harabim*, the merit of the community as a whole. He is certain that Klal Yisrael as a whole will receive a favorable judgment and, therefore, he should act b'simcha. Nevertheless, we fast on an individual basis because we fear for our own personal judgment. This one z'man, Erev Rosh Hashanah, reflects two separate ideas to focus on.

Let us make this Elul a meaningful time. Let's use its innate qualities to the fullest extent possible.

Always Trying to Grow

Success in life is something we all want to achieve. But what is the secret to success? What is the special ingredient needed in order to succeed in life?

Change. The ability to change—to reinvent oneself—is one thing that a person needs in order to reach his fullest potential. A person has to be open to change and strive to better himself throughout his life. Only then will he be successful and fulfilled.

Now that we know the formula for success, we only have to follow it! But change is one of the hardest things to do because we are all creatures of habit. Nobody likes change. We're satisfied with the status quo. Routine is safe and stable, while change is often seen as dangerous. Nevertheless, change is what we must do. As we say in the *Zichronos* on Rosh Hashanah, *"maasei adam ufkudaso,"* Hashem judges a person by his actions and by his station in life."

A person may be a Gaon Olam, an unbelievable genius. He might know all of Shas with Rashi, Tosfos and Poskim by heart. But if he has attained his knowledge because he has been blessed with a photographic memory, how much has he truly accomplished? He didn't really work that hard.

> Success is not only about where you end up; it's also about where you started.

Someone else might exert enormous efforts in diligent study, yet only succeed in being able to read Rashi script inside. He will merit reward in abundance. Success is not only about where you end up; it's also about where you started. If you started at the top and didn't go any further, you might look impressive, but you did not change. The one who started at the bottom, even if he has climbed only one rung, has truly succeeded. He has changed.

The Gemara in *Bava Basra* tells of an Amora who woke up from a trance in which he saw a vision of Olam Habah. "*Olam hafuch raisi*—I saw an upside-down world," he said. The *elyonim* were at the bottom and the *tachtonim* were on the top. People who we really thought were *elyonim*, people who impressed us, were on the bottom. Those who we thought of as lowly or simple people were on the top. Those "*elyonim*" were really not the successful ones, because they didn't *shteig*, they didn't grow. The more we change our nature, the more we add to what we are given, the more we succeed.

How can we make ourselves change? What instrument will give us the power to climb to the top? The Hebrew word for change is "*shinui*." Shin, Nun, Yud. What will give us the power for *shinui*? Learning Torah—"*Mishnah Torah*"—will give us the power to change. The word "*mishnah*" comes from the same root as "*shinui*."

The Gemara in *Kiddushin* discusses the wording of Shema and highlights the word "*v'shinantam*." The *Mishnah Berurah* tells us that although Shema can be said in any language, there are some words that do not translate into any other language. "*L'totafos*" is one of them and "*v'shinantam*" is another. The Gemara explains that "*v'shinantam*" connects to the word "*shen*," tooth, which is also from the same root as "*shinui*." What is the purpose of a tooth? To change food into a digestible substance that our bodies can handle. Returning to the word "*v'shinantam*," we can now present another explanation. "*V'shinantam*" comes from the word "*shinui*." "*V'shinantam l'vanecha*"—You should change your children with the lessons of the Torah.

The word "*yashan*," also from the same root, is used to describe something that is getting older. When something ages, it changes. The word for year, "*shana*," also comes from the root of change. The passing of time cannot occur without change. That is why Hashem is "*l'maalah min haz'man*—above the concept of time," because Hashem does not change.

It still may be hard for a person to change, even with this special instrument of limud haTorah. The reason for this is because we do not analyze our own faults. We are very quick to criticize others, but we do not recognize those flaws in ourselves. We build a protective wall around ourselves to shield our precious egos. In order to get through that wall, we need an even stronger dosage of limud haTorah. We need something that will shake us up and not only teach us Torah, but teach us how to live Torah. That something is Tochacha—Mussar, or rebuke. Rebuke will awaken within us the recognition of our faults and give us the push we need to change them. The pasuk in Mishlei tells us "*Hachazeik b'mussar, al teref; nitzreha ki hi chayecha*—Grab hold of Mussar, don't let go; cling to Mussar because it is the key to your life*"* (Mishlei 35:2).

Someone who does not change, who does not constantly

try to better himself, stagnates and deteriorates. He is not alive and vibrant. What enables us to change and better ourselves? Mussar. Sometimes, all a person needs is a flash, a bolt.

Nevuzaradan was the captain of Nevuchadnetzar's guard, and when he came to destroy the first Beis Hamikdash, he saw the blood of Zecharya the Navi bubbling in the place where he had been murdered. Nevuzaradan decided to avenge the Navi's death. He gathered the Sanhedrin and killed them all, but still the blood boiled. He gathered the Kohanim and murdered them, but still the blood boiled. He gathered innocent children and killed them, but the blood still boiled. He killed 94,000 Jews at one time. Then he called out to Hashem, " I've killed all the good ones. Isn't it enough? Do I have to kill them all?" Finally, the blood stopped boiling. Just then it hit Nevuzaradan with a flash. "If so many deaths were needed to atone for the murder of a single righteous man, how great will my punishment be ... I, who have murdered thousands?" In that instant, with that flash of Mussar, Nevuzaradan repented and became a *ger tzedek*.

Once, when I was a young boy, I was davening—and I was davening the way a small boy does. My uncle was watching me, and he came over and told me, "Forget the fact that you are speaking to the Ribono Shel Olam when you daven. Don't you want to pride yourself on the fact that everything you do, you do well?" Sometimes, all it takes is one flash of Mussar to start a change in you.

This concept of change is a unique and powerful human strength. The Mishnah in *Pirkei Avos* teaches us a very basic principle—anything in life that is important is attainable to everyone. *Ashirus* (wealth), therefore, does not mean having a million dollars, because not everyone can attain that. *Chachma* (wisdom) is not scoring 200 on a 1Q test. And *Gevura* (strength) does not mean lifting tremendous weights.

How can we explain these three attributes in a way that they are equally attainable to everyone? *Ashirus* means being happy with what you have. *Chachma* means learning from everyone. And *Gevura* is conquering your passions. One who has the ability to suppress the flaws in his nature, to change, is one who is invested with *koach*, strength. And that is why the root of Tochacha is "*koach*." The power of rebuke gives us the power to change.

The Baalei Mussar tell us that one of the best ways to drive home a message is to keep repeating it, to keep on learning about it. We see this in the common Talmudic expressions, "*margela b'fumei*—a pearl in his mouth," and "*hu haya omeir*—he would always say." The saying would be *ragil* (regularly) on his lips. He would constantly say it. This idea holds true for us as well. By learning and repeating the sayings of Chazal, they will become a part of us. Once they are a part of us, we will start acting upon them. We will change ourselves.

We should realize that we cannot change completely overnight. If we try too much at once, we will not be able to do it. Hashem just wants to see a turn, a slight change. If we show that we want to change, even if we change only a little, then Hashem will bring us the rest of the way. "*Habah l'tahair, m'sayin oso*— One who comes to purify himself is given heavenly assistance." That can help us achieve a lot in a short time.

Now we know that the key to success is change. By changing and bettering ourselves, we can reach our highest goals. We also know what gives us the ability to change: limud haTorah—studying, learning and taking one's learning to heart. If we use Torah methods to change ourselves, then we are sure to achieve true success in life.

Emotional Somersaults

How wondrous the human mind is! Our minds are capable of handling emotional somersaults! If you have ever experienced going to a bris in the morning, followed by a funeral in the afternoon and capped off by a wedding in the evening, you know what I mean!

We have many occasions where we must practice mental gymnastics. In the unfortunate event that one loses a close relative the day before a festival, one is expected to get up from shiva after just one day, and enter into the Yom Tov with joyousness. One of the mitzvos of Shabbos is to shut out all our weekday preoccupations as soon as we usher in the holy day. On Shabbos, we change our mindsets from Chol to Kodesh. Tefillah is another example. When it's time to daven, a Jew is expected to shift mental gears. The telephone, clients and all other mundane pursuits recede in the background as we take three steps forward and enter the palace of Hashem.

This ability to "ride" the emotional roller coaster is certainly challenged when we tackle the month of Elul, which includes Rosh Hashanah, Aseres Y'mei Teshuvah and Yom Kippur. We leave the relatively lazy, carefree days of summer and mentally catapult into the most critical period of the year. The transition must be made from swimming pools, barbecuing and ball playing, to the sudden tensions of bus stops, orientations and homework, and all of this coupled with early morning Selichos. We are obligated to start a schedule of sincere soul-searching and bring thoughts of teshuvah to the forefront. It is truly a Herculean task! But we are up to it. Hashem never asks from us more than we can handle!

The month of Av is an abbreviation for Edom and Bavel, the two nationalities that brought about the destruction of the two Temples. The month of Elul also stands for the middle words in the verse, "*Umal Hashem Elokecha es l'vavcha v'es levav zarecha*—Hashem will circumcise (cut away the evil section) of your hearts and the hearts of your children" (Devarim 30:6). The words, "*Es l'vavcha v'es levav*," your hearts and your children's hearts, emphasize that in Elul our efforts at self-improvement and repentance should be so obvious that it should impact even on our children!

One of the powerful weapons of the Yetzer Hara is to confuse us into thinking that we don't really need to do teshuvah. This kind of thinking is helped by the natural tendency of "*Ein adam roeh nigay atzmo*—A person doesn't see his own faults." This attitude, however, is extremely dangerous! The *Or Yecheskel* asks a strong question. We know that if one embarrasses someone publicly to the point that his face drains of blood, it is as if he murdered him and he loses his Afterlife. Yet, in the case of an actual murder, capital punishment is demanded, but the murderer keeps his eternal reward. Why is this? The *Or Yecheskel* explains that when one embarrasses a person, one is not consumed with guilt and contrition, and it is less likely one will be motivated to do teshuvah. Therefore, when one embarrasses his neighbor, he may lose his Afterlife as well. The point is that it can be lethal to think that one doesn't need to do teshuvah.

The author of *Darchei Mussar* relates that one Rosh Chodesh Elul he was walking out of his shul with one of his members and mentioned, "It's Elul and time to do teshuvah." The man responded that he was already 63 years old and didn't have much to repent for. The *Darchei Mussar* answered, "The great Rabbeinu Nissim used to say the following Viduy (confession): 'Hashem, if I would itemize my sins and explain them, I would run out of breath and not finish my account!' And you, sir, say you have little to do teshuvah for?" The saintly Chofetz Chaim was heard to say on his 84th birthday, "Yisrael Meir, you are 84 today and still have not done teshuvah. What will be with you?!"

> The Chofetz Chaim was heard to say on his 84th birthday, "Yisrael Meir, you are 84 today and still have not done teshuvah. What will be with you?!"

Pharaoh stated, "I sinned this time. Hashem is righteous and I and my nation are wicked." The monstrous Pharaoh, who bathed in the blood of 300 Jewish babies daily, who buried children alive in the walls of Pis'om and Raamses and who enslaved 600,000 people for over a century, actually conceded that he had sinned. However, while he admitted his sin, he only accepted blame for "this time" and used the phrase "*chatasi*," which connotes inadvertent sin. Such arrogance! The Ra"n and the Chofetz Chaim are full of sin, while Pharaoh made only one mistake! The implication is clear: The greater the person, the more aware they are of their shortcomings!

An effective technique of the Evil Inclination is to make us painfully aware that we don't keep our teshuvah commitments for long. He shows us that we are basically making the same promises year after year. The Yetzer Hara then whispers to us, "Why bother? You're not going to stick with it anyway." He persists. "With all your faults, you made it through this year. So you're not any worse than last year. Why worry?" This, however, is far from the truth. Who knows? We may have made it through the year only "by the skin of our teeth," barely hanging on to the threads of some ancestral merits!

As to the meaningfulness of teshuvah that might not last, let's look again to Pharaoh. For saying the statement, "*Chatasi hapa'am*," Rashi in Beshalach (Shemos 16:12) informs us that all of Pharaoh's people who drowned in the Red Sea merited burial. Now, how long did Pharaoh's contrition last? When the plague was stopped, he promptly returned to his stubborn ways. Yet, he was awarded a permanent reward for a very temporary contrition.

In a similar vein, the *Kad HaKemach* teaches us that the meaning of the 13th attribute of mercy, *V'nakay* (to be clean), means that if one does teshuvah sincerely for a sin, he is permanently clean from that sin, even if at a later date he slips back into the bad habit!

So we have to persevere. We may have to navigate many twists and turns, but with effort, we can focus clearly and purify ourselves through teshuvah.

The Daily Challenges of the Yetzer Hara

It is imperative that we never underestimate the power of our Evil Inclination, as it is always a mistake of the highest order to make light of a true enemy. If you've been thinking lately that life's temptations are really not that difficult, think again.

The Gemara teaches us, "*Yitzro shel adam misgabeir alav bechol yom um'vakeish hamiso, v'ilmalei Hakadosh Baruch Hu ozro, eino yachol lo*—A person's Yetzer Hara prevails upon him every day and tries to kill him, and if Hashem wouldn't give him Divine assistance, he would not be able to overcome it" (*Kiddushin* 30b). Thus, we see that it is not naturally possible to control ourselves without the help of Hashem.

With this realization, we include in our daily prayers many requests for Hashem's help in this battle. One of the first times in the day that we petition for this support is in the prayer we say before donning our tefillin. There, we say, "… *shelo yisgareh banu Yetzer Hara, v'yanicheinu la'avod es Hashem ka'asher im l'vaveinu*—that the Evil Inclination should not provoke us and that it should permit us to serve Hashem as we want to in our hearts." Rav Moshe Feinstein, *zt"l*, once told me that we can see from the choice of the wording, "as we want to in our hearts," that our hearts are innately good and upright. Therefore, it is merely our job not to allow the Yetzer Hara to distract us and deter us from our natural goodness.

The next time we pray for success against the lure of the Yetzer Hara is in the *"vihi ratzon"* of the bracha *"HaMaavir Sheina."* Surprisingly, this blessing contains two very similar requests concerning the Yetzer Hara. First, we ask, *"Al yishlot banu Yetzer Hara*—Don't let our Yetzer Hara rule over us." Then, soon after, we say, *"V'chof es yitzreinu lehishtabed lach*—Subdue our [evil] inclination to be subservient to You." How unusual! It seems as if we are making the same request twice in one blessing.

The *Siach Yitzchak* gives a marvelous explanation. The Yetzer Hara has two separate missions to accomplish. First, it is his job to ensure that we always have *bechirah* (free will). When we get to the next world (the Afterlife) and enjoy its eternal bliss, Hashem wants us to really enjoy it, and not to be embarrassed that our reward is *"nahama d'kisufa,"* bread of shame. We should not feel that we are getting freebies, but that our reward was well deserved. Therefore, the Yetzer Hara provides us with daily challenges and is the vehicle that enables us to confront our daily pursuit of *"uvacharta b'chaim,"* choosing life.

But the Yetzer Hara also has an entirely different mission. The Yetzer Hara must also ensure that we take care of our physical needs with diligence. The Gemara teaches us that when the Anshei Knesses HaGedolah prayed to rid the world of the Yetzer Hara for idolatry, they attempted to do the same with the Yetzer Hara for lust. The result, however, was surprising. The next day, there were no newly hatched eggs in the entire world. There was no progress, no procreation. Thus, we learn that without the passion for pleasure that we naturally possess, we would neglect many of the daily actions that are necessary to keep the world running. Without our innate passions, we would not be drawn to eat, drink, sleep or reproduce. The world would die out.

Now, says the *Siach Yitzchak*, we can understand why we say two separate prayers concerning the Evil One. First, we ask, "*Al yishlot banu*—Do not let him control us." This refers to his job of trying to provoke us to sin. We ask Hashem to assist us in preventing the Yetzer Hara from overpowering our better senses. Then, when it comes to the Yetzer Hara's other mission—ensuring that our physical component is well taken care of—we pray that our passions be channeled in the right direction and be subjugated to Hashem's will. Thus, we pray that our sleep should cause us to have more patience in the morning with our loved ones and better concentration during davening. We daven that our eating and drinking should strengthen us and enable us to better serve Hashem. It's our hope that all the other physical actions we do will help us toward our spiritual avodah.

In addition to asking for help, we thank Hashem for His daily assistance in dealing with the Yetzer Hara. Every day, in the morning blessings, we exclaim, "*Ozer Yisrael bigvurah*—Hashem girds Yisrael with might." The Gemara links this blessing to the action of putting on our belt in the morning. Now, this is somewhat puzzling. What does donning a belt have to do with strength? The common explanation is that in the olden days, the scabbard with its sword was worn on the belt much like today's gun and holster. The belt, therefore, symbolized might and physical prowess.

This explanation, however, does not seem to fit the

bill. If this blessing refers to a physical attribute, why is it reserved for Yisrael? Indeed, most of the other blessings do not include the word Yisrael since Hashem daily opens the eyes, straightens the posture and directs the footsteps of all men. It seems that in this blessing regarding strength, using the word Yisrael, we must be referring to something uniquely Jewish. I would, therefore, like to suggest that in this blessing we are thanking Hashem for girding us with the ability to successfully battle our Evil Inclination. After all, this is how we define true might in *Pirkei Avos*. As we have learned, "*Aizehu gibor, hakovesh es yitzro*—Who is mighty? He who conquers his passions."

It is worthwhile to note that in defining spiritual might, the Tanna emphasizes it is one who conquers "his" passions. Too many of us judge our overall success by comparing ourselves to those around us. When we see that we are not miserly like Chaim, or that we don't berate our spouses like Rochel, we pat ourselves on the back and assume that we are doing quite all right. But this is a serious error. Our success in life can only be measured by how we conquer *our own* temptations. Each of us has our own vulnerabilities and weak spots, and we must work on them.

> Our success in life can only be measured by how we conquer our own temptations.

It is very worthwhile to make a Cheshbon Hanefesh, a personal examination of the areas in which our Yetzer Hara does battle with us. Perhaps it is in the arena of Torah neglect, talking in shul or being insensitive to our neighbor's feelings. Maybe our weaknesses can be found at the workplace in the way we deal with co-workers, employees or employers. How are our business ethics and our commercial integrity? Only when we identify what our passions are—and successfully combat them—can we truly feel that we are spiritually mighty.

Another place where we pray to Hashem to help us be victorious against our Evil Inclination is in the blessing of *"Ahava Raba/Ahavas Olam"* before Kriyas Shema. There, we ask Hashem for the understanding and intellect *"lishmor v'laasos,"* to heed His negative commands and to fulfill His positive ones. In the wonderful prayer of *"U'va L'Tzion,"* we petition Hashem *"l'hachein l'vavam eilecha—*to direct our hearts to You." The word *l'vavam* is written using two *"bais"*es to indicate that we are charged with serving Hashem with "both" our hearts—both our good and evil inclinations. This emphasizes the hope that both our inclinations, even our base and evil tendencies, should be channeled to the service of Hashem.

In the merit of our learning Torah together, may we be *zocheh* to successfully conquer our personal Yetzer Haras and channel our entire being to attaining higher spirituality.

Combating the Force of Habit

Every day, in our morning prayers, we ask Hashem, "*V'dabeik libeinu b'mitzvosecha*—May our hearts be attached to Your commandments." This is an especially important tefillah for the religious-from-birth Jew, because one who is accustomed to doing the mitzvos repetitively since early child-hood is threatened by the danger of habit, monotony and routine. Thus, we ask Hashem to attach our hearts to His mitzvos.

> We must serve Hashem not like robots, but with our full heart.

We want to be able to do mitzvos in a heartfelt and passionate way. In a similar vein, we daven, "*Ashrei ish sheyishma l'mitzvosecha, v'Sorasecha u'dvarecha yasim al libo*—Fortunate is he who listens to Your commandments and who puts Your Torah and Your words upon his heart." Once again, this echoes our sentiment that the proper way to serve Hashem is not with mere robot-like actions, but through the medium of the heart.

One of the ways to combat the threat of habitual religiosity is to learn more about the reasons and significance of our mitzvos. When we know the deeper meaning of our precepts, it is easier to do them with a zest and a passion.

One example of a mitzvah that may lose its freshness over time is the mitzvah of tzitzis. Since men wear tzitzis

365 days a year, it is one of the most repetitive mitzvos we have. We tend to put on our tzitzis early in the morning, before we've cleared the cobwebs of sleep from our minds. An injection of understanding regarding this critical mitzvah can make a real difference in our proper fulfillment of it.

When we don the tallis katan, we make the bracha, "*L'hisateif batzitzis.*" The first two letters of these words are Lamed and Bais. Numerically combined, these two letters add up to 32, which is the amount of threads on the tzitzis (four tzitzis times eight threads). The *Sefer Haz'chirah* says that thinking about one's tzitzis is a segulah to protect one's self from toothaches. Just as there are 32 threads on our tzitzis, we reach maturity with 32 teeth in our mouths. (cf. *Midrash Talpios*, quoted by Rav Chaim Kanievsky, *shlit"a*, which says that Jewish people have 32 teeth while many other nationalities have only 31 teeth.) This segulah is mentioned in the *Kavanos Ha-Arizal* as well. Additionally, the Arizal says that focusing on the corner of one's tzitzis is beneficial to protecting one from the temptations of anger. He supports this statement by pointing out that the word for corner in Hebrew is "*kanaf*." The gematria of *kanaf* is 150, and this is the numerical equivalent of "*kaas*" (anger). The Arizal also says that by looking at the tzitzis during Kriyas Shema, one protects himself from going blind. Rav Moshe Feinstein, *zt"l*, would bring his tzitzis right next to his eyes when saying "*ur'isem oso*" in the morning Kriyas Shema.

As we know, the mitzvah of tzitzis is a symbol of all of the 613 commandments. We say in our Kriyas Shema, "*U'risem oso u'zechartem es kol mitzvos Hashem*—You will see it (the tzitzis) and remember *all* of Hashem's mitzvos." The gematria of tzitzis is 600, and when we add this to the five knots and eight threads on each corner, we get a total of 613.

Unfortunately, today we cannot fulfill many of the 613 mitzvos. Here in *Chutz la'Aretz*, we are bereft of the opportunity of fulfilling such mitzvos as *terumah*, *maaser* and *shmittah*. Even the fortunate residents of Eretz Yisrael cannot bring *korbanos* and *nesachim* (sacrifices and wine offerings) since, because of our many sins, we do not have our Temple. Many of us will never get a chance to fulfill such mitzvos as *shiluach hakan* (sending away the mother bird) or building a parapet. However, Hashem gave us a special device to have a portion in all of the mitzvos. When we put on our tzitzis in the morning and hold them over our head, we should think as follows: "These tzitzis symbolize and represent all 613 commandments. Hashem, I really want to be able to do all of these mitzvos—to make *aliya l'regel*, visit the Temple three times a year, bring a *korban shlamim*, *olah* and *menachos* (a burnt offering, a peace offering and all kinds of meal offerings), but I am unable to." With this daily thought, Hashem will consider it as if we truly fulfilled these mitzvos, for the Gemara teaches us, *"Chishev la'asos mitzvah v'ne'enas v'lo asa'ah, ma'aleh alav hakasuv k'ilu asa'ah*—if a person plans to do a mitzvah but is unable to do so because of circumstances beyond his control, Hashem considers it as if he did it" (*Brachos* 6a).

So there you have it—a whole potpourri of new thoughts that we can have when we put on our tzitzis! One morning, we could zoom in on really wanting to fulfill *shmittah*. The next morning, we can wish we were able to do *nisuch hamayim*, the water libation performed on Sukkos. Whether it's thinking about a collage of ancient mitzvos, extra teeth protection (besides your daily brushing) or protecting one from anger and blindness, these are just some thoughts to add a little bounce to our mitzvah of tzitzis. Hopefully, these ideas will protect us so that we do not fall into the trap of "*mitzvos anashim m'lumadah*," just doing the mitzvos by rote, without feeling.

One of the reasons why we hear the shofar in shul every morning in Elul, says the *K'sav Sofer*, is to remind ourselves, "*shapru maaseichem*—to beautify our deeds." What better way to make our mitzvos prettier in the eyes of Hashem than to dress them up with meaningful thoughts? May it be the will of Hashem that we succeed in attaching our heart to all His mitzvos.

Making Every Act Count

Students of Torah are well aware that there is nothing superfluous in the language of the Torah. Every phrase comes to teach us a myriad of lessons. Therefore, when the Torah says, *"Vayeitzei Yaakov miB'er Sheva vayeileich Charanah—And Yaakov left the city of Be'er Sheva and went to Charan"* (Bereishis 28:10), Rashi immediately wonders why it didn't simply say, *"Vayeileich Yaakov Charanah—and Yaakov traveled to Charan."* The *Beis Halevi* gives a beautiful explanation. He says that Yaakov actually had a double mission. First, he was leaving his home on the instructions of his mother Rivka, to escape the danger of his vengeful brother Esav. Second, he was simultaneously embarking on the journey to the house of Lavan in Charan to find a wife—to fulfill the directive of his father Yitzchak. This explains the pasuk perfectly, for Yaakov *left* Be'er Sheva to escape the wrath of Esav, and he *went* to Charan to find a mate.

This is not simply a historical vignette. Rather, it is teaching us a very important principle for living. Any action one does can be, in reality, a fulfillment of not just one mitzvah—but a whole series of mitzvos. In our day and age, when multi-tasking has become a way of life, this is a concept into which we can really sink our teeth.

> A single action can potentially fulfill many mitzvos, if only we have the proper intentions.

Let's take a simple example: One gets up in the morning and washes his face. If he's a thinking Jew, he immediately realizes that he is preparing himself for prayer—to speak with God. Therefore, washing his face is a fulfillment of the directive, "*Hikon likras Elokecha Yisrael*—Prepare properly to greet your God, O Israel" (Amos 4:12). Upon further reflection, if he is married, he is also making himself look suitable for his spouse; a fulfillment of "*v'simach es ishto*—to cause one's wife to rejoice" (Devarim 24:5). If we stretch this a little further, there is yet a third mitzvah that one fulfills by washing the face. Man is created in the image of Hashem, and when he washes his face, he is giving honor to Hashem. As the Midrash explains, when someone washes his face, it's as if he is polishing the "image" of Hashem.

Let's take another example: Someone sits down to eat a meal. The first mitzvah that comes to mind is "*V'nishmartem me'od l'nafshoseichem*" (Devarim 4:46), the positive commandment of watching our health very carefully. We are required to treat our bodies with care and respect. There is an additional aspect to eating. There's the old saying: Some people make a bracha in order to eat; others eat in order to make a bracha. Most of us are not on so lofty a level that we eat for the sole purpose of earning the mitzvah of a bracha. However, we can definitely have in mind that our eating is both a pleasure and an opportunity to do a mitzvah. When reciting the Birchas HaMazon, one can bear in mind that this bracha is a fulfillment of a precious biblical commandment. When we allow our eating to be a means for blessing and thanking Hashem, as well as a means of sustaining the body that Hashem has blessed us with, we have doubled our mitzvah activity.

Let's take this idea still further. Let's say one plans to learn Torah, or daven, or take care of the children, or go to work to support one's family, or engage in a *shalom bayis* activity. When one sits down to eat beforehand, if he has eaten with the intention that the meal will fortify him to have more strength, enthusiasm and patience for the task ahead, then this meal becomes a *hechsher mitzvah*, a preparatory act for doing a mitzvah. It is an accessory to the learning or davening or familial task. There is a well-known Talmudic dictum, *"Hechsher mitzvah k'mitzvah*—The preparatory act of a mitzvah is like the mitzvah itself." Thus, the very act of eating becomes an extension of the Torah learning, prayer, child-rearing or shalom bayis activity.

There are other potential lofty goals in the act of eating. When we enjoy our Shabbos food in honor of Hashem Who created the world, it becomes an affirmation of our belief in the Creator. When we eat with the proper intentions during festivals or at any one of the vast array of seudos mitzvah (meals in honor of a specific mitzvah), such as a bris, pidyon haben, bar mitzvah or wedding, we are performing many mitzvos at once.

Let's bear in mind that these are only two simple examples. The message is one that applies to all our actions throughout the day and night. The pasuk tells us, *"B'chol derachecha da'eihu, v'hu y'yasher orchosecha*—In all your ways acknowledge Him, and He will set your path straight" (Mishlei 3:6). May it be the will of Hashem that we learn to conduct all the various aspects of our lives wisely and meaningfully.

The Torah Way to Go to Sleep

When preparing for Rosh Hashanah and Yom Kippur, many people concentrate upon character refinement. They might work hard to improve their anger control, struggle mightily to stamp out forbidden feelings of hate and jealousy or try to purge sinful thoughts from their minds. All of these pursuits are wonderful and absolutely necessary, but I would like to focus on another aspect of personal improvement: bettering our actual day-to-day religious behavior.

Let's use as an example how we get ready to go to sleep in the evening. The *Mishnah Berurah* strongly recommends that we make a personal accounting, a Cheshbon Hanefesh, before we retire every night. He suggests that we review the day's events and scrutinize whether we tripped up with such sins as lying, mockery or speaking *lashon hara*. He urges us to make a careful daily audit in the area of bitul Torah, neglecting Torah study.

> The Mishnah Berurah strongly recommends that we make a personal accounting, a Cheshbon Hanefesh, before we retire every night.

Numerous other reflections are possible, too. Did we daven with a minyan? Did we pay attention to our prayers? Did we make brachos properly and answer *Amein* correctly? We might also add the following personal question: Did we invest sufficiently in our Olam Habah, our Afterlife, on this particular and irreplaceable day? While this may seem like a lot to do when we are on the verge of collapse and ready to turn in for the night, with some practice it can be done quickly and can be very rewarding.

The Chofetz Chaim, zt"l, adds that we should forgive anyone who wronged us or caused us pain throughout the day. He writes that in the merit of doing this, we will earn long life. Forgiving everyone may seem easier said than done, but a long life is worth some effort and hardship. The Zohar, in Parshas Mikeitz, teaches us that one who sincerely forgives those who have wronged him—and instead takes steps to do good toward them—will be saved from death.

Every Torah Jew, including busy men and women and tired boys and girls, should say at least the first chapter of Kriyas Shema before going to sleep. It is preferable to say all three parshiyos of Shema together with the words "Kel Melech Ne'eman," for together they total 248 words, which correspond to the 248 limbs of the body and affords them special nightly protection. The nighttime blessing of Hamapil should also be said whenever possible. It is said that the saintly Satmar Rebbe, R' Yoel Teitelbaum, zt"l, took more time saying Kriyas Shema al Hamitah and the bracha of Hamapil than the amount of time that he actually slept!

Let us take note of the fact that about one third of our lives are spent in sleep. After 120 years, when Hashem judges us, most of us will draw a blank for all of the time we spent sleeping. Since, after all, we didn't do mitzvos while we were snoring away in our beds, these hours of our lives will have been fruitless. However, with just a little nightly attention, we can convert a full one-third of our lives into dynamic mitzvah production. Again, we refer to the Halachic rule that "*Hechsher mitzvah k'mitzvah*—The preparatory act of a mitzvah is like the mitzvah itself." Therefore, before we lie down and go to sleep for the night, we should contemplate or even verbalize that we are going to sleep so that we can daven better and learn with greater concentration the next day. Then, our sleep becomes a *hechsher mitzvah* for davening and Torah study.

If, before retiring, a woman focuses on the fact that her sleep will enable her to be more patient with her children in the morning, and fresh and full of vigor for her family, she converts her sleep into a chinuch activity and a shalom bayis endeavor.

If we take this approach, then hopefully when we get up to Shamayim, we will be able to show how we spent all our years with one hundred percent productivity.

Wrapping Up the Year Right

Elul is the last month of the Jewish year. In Yiddishkeit, this concept assumes significant prominence.

We are taught, *"Hakol holeich achar hachesom—* Everything goes according to the finale"* (*Brachos* 14). Endings are important. The ending of a matter is a reflection of all the time and effort that went into it. A good ending is a springboard for a new and fresh beginning. An example of this concept is found in our Sukkos prayers. When Sukkos falls on Shabbos, we say, *"Hoshannah, yosheves u'mamtenes ad klos haShabbos, Hoshannah,"* which means, "Please save us, in the merit of our sitting and waiting until the end of Shabbos, please save us." This is a rather strange petition. Is it meritorious that people sit and look at their watches, waiting until Shabbos has ended? Rather, I think this prayer signifies that it is the final moments of Shabbos that are the most critical. In fact, the character and integrity of the entire Shabbos are defined in these last moments. So, too, since Elul is the final month of the year, it affords us an incredible opportunity to correct and refine our entire year.

There are, of course, a myriad of ways to do this and each of us has his or her individual strengths and weaknesses to consider. I would like to focus on one area that could greatly improve our chances for a beautiful New Year. This is the area of *shmiras halashon*—guarding one's tongue. We all know the famous dictum: *"Mi ha'ish hechofetz chaim* ... —Who wants life? Guard your tongue from speaking evil" (Tehillim 44:13). Since Elul is the time of the year when we petition Hashem for life and happiness, it is clear that we must reevaluate our manner of speech and work to improve it.

In a most astonishing statement, the Vilna Gaon revealed (in the *Iggeres HaGra*, the letter he wrote to his family before he departed for Eretz Yisrael) the vital importance of guarding our tongue. He writes that the most powerful factor in determining our Olam Habah is proper speech. This is such an awesome statement and such a fundamental life-lesson that it's astounding that it doesn't grace everyone's refrigerator and office desk! Similarly, the *Yerushalmi* in *Pe'ah* says that just as Torah is equal to all mitzvos, so, too, *lashon hara* is equal to all the aveiros.

The Satan uses the sin of *lashon hara* to convict us in judgment. The Zohar reveals that the Satan cannot prosecute us on his own. The Torah says, "*Al pi shenayim eidim yakum davar*—Evidence can be established only with two witnesses" (Devarim 19:15). So how does the Satan corroborate his accusations? Here is an example. Let's suppose that Shmuel talks a lot during davening. The Satan wants to prosecute him, but can't do it by himself. However, he hears that there is a chasanah at El Carib and decides to attend. He hovers around the smorgasbord and listens to the swirls of conversation. Suddenly, he hears Chaim telling someone how terrible it is

> If we avoid speaking badly about others, Hashem won't listen to the bad things others might say about us.

that Shmuel is always talking in shul. "What a crass fellow!" Chaim says. "I don't know why the Rabbi puts up with it!" The Satan pounces on this opportunity—now he has the partner he needs to prosecute Shmuel. Thus, Chaim's sinful chatter actually caused punishment to descend upon another Jew.

The Zohar continues: The Satan doesn't stop there. He asks Hashem, "Since Chaim helped me prosecute another Jew, can I, measure for measure, now audit Chaim's records to see if he's due for any prosecution?" And Hashem allows it. Thus, we see how imperative it is for us to avoid speaking ill about each other, especially so close to the judgment day of Rosh Hashanah. By not speaking and listening to *lashon hara* about others, we gain powerful protection. As an aspect of *middah k'neged middah* (*Shabbos* 105), Hashem won't listen to any bad things people may say about us.

Let's strengthen our "talking" muscles for the good. Let's use our power of speech to bring us closer to Hakadosh Baruch Hu. Mothers should commit themselves to using wise and encouraging words to enhance the Torah environment in their homes. Wives should motivate their husbands toward Torah excellence by articulating their pride and happiness with their spouse's Torah accomplishments. A resolution to learn the meaning of our prayers (the study of which is also considered Torah learning) and saying them more clearly is a powerful commitment to bring before the Kisei HaKavod (the throne of Glory) on the Day of Judgment.

In the merit of our attempt at self-improvement and our trying to avoid the pitfalls of the Yetzer Hara, may all of our efforts prove successful.

More Effective and Powerful Prayer

Sometimes, it seems as if there is no good news. The financial world always seems to be in flux. Terrorism threatens us abroad and in our homes and schools. Our own Jewish community suffers with the trials of kids-at-risk, older singles, infertility and instability in our educational system.

This smorgasbord of woes fills one with dismay. What does the Torah Jew do to deal with these problems?

The pasuk in Tehillim answers succinctly, *"Min hameitzar karasi Kah*—From distress I call out to God"* (Tehillim 118:5). Similarly, another verse states, *"Tefillah l'ani chi ya'atof*—A prayer of the needy when he feels faint"* (Tehillim 102:1). Indeed, the entire theme of Dovid Hamelech's Tehillim is that prayer is the correct Jewish response to life's troubles. Clutching the tear-stained pages of Tehillim, Jews have trustingly looked to Hashem for salvation throughout the ages. During crusades and inquisitions, pogroms and expulsions, Holocaust and war, we Jews turn to Hashem in prayer. As we gird ourselves to energize our prayers, let's discuss some important concepts about tefillah.

To succeed at prayer, the first principle that one needs to work on is to internalize that one is actually conversing with Hashem. While intellectually this sounds elementary, in reality, many people talk to the siddur or the bentcher instead of focusing on the One Above. This is more common with Americans who don't speak Hebrew and must actively translate the prayer in order to understand their prayers. Many people, due to lack of time, distraction, laziness or habit, simply skip this step and say the words of prayer without meaning at all. So once again, a crucial first step in successful prayer is to heighten our awareness that we are talking to Hashem.

A crucial first step in successful prayer is to heighten our awareness that we are actually talking to Hashem.

Once we reach this big milestone, the next step is to strengthen our belief that when we pray correctly, it really will help to improve our lives. Many people have a lackadaisical attitude toward their prayers. This is in part due to the fact that they don't realize what a great improvement they can make in the quality of their lives by praying properly. In our Shemoneh Esrei liturgy, we state clearly, "*Ki Atah shomei'a tefilas kol peh amcha Yisrael*—For You listen to the prayers of *all* of Your nation Israel." Hashem is listening to us. If we pray sincerely and meaningfully, we can greatly enhance the happiness and success of our lives and the lives around us.

Keep in mind Whom you are speaking to—when you get up in the morning, when you eat and when you go to sleep. Hashem is there and He is listening.

Thinking While We Pray Makes All the Difference

We live in a world of a variety of routine medical tests—CT scans and MRIs, colonoscopies and PAP smears, mammograms and prostate screenings. These are only a few that we are all familiar with. While these tests are a great gift to mankind—helping to detect potentially dangerous diseases before advancing beyond control—they are also very scary and create many a fearful moment in the lives of modern day men and women. The Torah teaches us, "*Va'avad'tem eis Hashem Elokeichem uveirach es lachm'cha v'es meimecha vahasirosi machalah mikirbecha; Lo sih'yeh mishakeilah vaakarah b'artzecha; es mispar yamecha amalei*— And you should serve Hashem your God and He will bless your bread and your water; He will remove sickness from your midst. No one will bury their children in their lifetime. You will be spared barrenness in your land and I will fulfill the quota of your years" (Shemos 23:25-26). This pasuk, besides promising us Divine assistance toward our sustenance and a host of other assurances, guarantees us removal of any sickness from our midst. This is the kind of medical insurance that we hope for—and it is provided to us by paying the premium mentioned in the beginning of the pasuk, "*Va'avad'tem eis Hashem Elokeichem*—Work for Hashem your God."

What is exactly the nature of this work that provides us with such Divine assurances? The *Sefer HaIkarim* states that this pasuk is referring to the work of prayer. The Gemara teaches us in the beginning of *Maseches Taanis* (2b), "*Eizehu avodah she'hi b'leiv? Hevei omer zu tefillah*—What is the work of the heart? We conclude that it is prayer." In a similar fashion, the *Baal HaTurim* points out that most of the fifty-three directives in Parshas Mishpatim are written in the singular. Thus, it says, "*Lo sishtachave*—You should not bow down (to their idols), *v'lo saav'deim*—You should not worship them (idols)" (Shemos 20:5), all written in the singular. However, in our verse, the word "*va'avad'tem*" is written in the plural. The *Baal HaTurim* explains that the verse refers to prayer, and the most effective form of prayer is to join in a minyan—to pray amongst the many. Thus, the word *va'avad'tem* is written here in the plural. The next question is: What exactly is the nature of the work of prayer? The Avudraham, *zt"l*, in his preface to the Shemoneh Esrei, writes that the work of prayer is "*l'hasir hamachashavah hatrudah b'iskei haolam u'l'haviah b'shibud hakavanah*—to remove thoughts that are occupied with the mundane affairs of the world and to focus our concentration on our devotion to Hashem." Thus, we see that all the aforementioned Divine promises come to those who diligently apply themselves to proper kavanah during davening. The Avudraham caps this with an incredible gematria. The word tefillah numerically equals 515. He reveals that the words "*b'kavanas haleiv*," with the concentration of the heart, also equal exactly 515.

The realization of how critical it is to clear our minds of worldly thoughts while we pray highlights how talking in shul clashes with the whole objective of the work of prayer. While the devoted worshiper is working hard at the avodah of purging the thoughts of daily living from his or her mind, others are actively engaged in discussing life's trivialities. The *Chovos Halevavos* makes the powerful declaration that prayer without kavanah is like the peel without the fruit, like a body without a soul. The *Hafla'ah* takes this statement of the *Chovos Halevavos* a step further. He elaborates that since we want our prayers to rise to the Heavens, they must be infused with a ruach, a spirit, that causes them to levitate all the way to the Kisei HaKavod, Hashem's Throne of Glory. The *Chovos Halevavos* says that prayer without kavanah is like a body without spirit. Such prayers are lifeless and cannot rise to the Heavens. It is only when we inject kavanah into our prayers that we fill them with the necessary spirit to cause them to soar and pierce the very Heavens where they can be most effective.

> Prayer without kavanah is like the peel without the fruit, like a body without a soul.

With the help of Hashem, may we be inspired to pray with full kavanah and, in that merit, may we earn all the promises offered to us—that of being spared from all sickness, being granted Divine help in our parnassa and being granted a long life of happiness.

The Making of a Minyan

One of the hallowed rituals in the Beis Hamikdash was the offering of the sweet smelling k'tores, the savory incense.

This concoction was prepared using a special Divine recipe. The Torah dictates that it was created from eleven specific spices. We can imagine that—since God is the Creator of all spices and this mixture was to be the very special fragrance to be used in His Temple—the most perfect composition was devised for the *k'tores*. Surprisingly though, one of the eleven spices was *chelbenah*, galbanum, which has a very foul aroma. The Gemara in *Maseches Kerisos* (6b) comments on the odd selection of the galbanum and extrapolates a fundamental concept of Yiddishkeit. The beautiful scent of the *k'tores* must include the foul-smelling galbanum. The *poshei Yisrael*, our sinners, must be included in our prayers and during our fast days. In each case, the result is whole and good.

The word that describes a Jewish congregation is the Hebrew word "*tzibbur.*" This word is an acronym for **tzaddikim**, **beinonim** and **reshaim**. The true Jewish congregation is a blend of the righteous, the average and the wicked. A similar lesson is taught concerning the mitzvah of the four species we shake on the Sukkos festival. The Gemara informs us about the aravah, the willow, *"Ein ba lo tam v'lo rei'ach*—It has neither taste nor fragrance." Though it offers no taste or smell, we must bind it together with the other species and only then is the mitzvah complete. On Yom Kippur, the holiest day of the year, we say the moving prayer of Kol Nidre. Before he begins, the chazzan states, "*Anu matirin l'hispallel im ha-avaryanim*—We permit ourselves to pray with the transgressors." This is a very delicate issue. On the one hand, every day we beseech Hashem, "*Harchikeinu mei'adam ra*—Distance us from the bad person." *Pirkei Avos* states that when Rabban Yochanan sent out his disciples to discover what was the worst trait to avoid, one came back with the answer "*chaver ra*, a bad friend." Another answered "*shachein ra*, a bad neighbor." So, too, we are taught "*Oy l'rasha v'oy lishcheino*—Woe to the wicked and woe to his neighbor." In addition, in the very first chapter of Tehillim, it says, "*Ashrei ha'ish asher lo halach b'atzas reshaim … uv'moshav leitzim lo yashav*—Fortunate is the one who does not follow the advice of the wicked … and does not sit in an assemblage of scoffers" (Tehillim 1:1).

So, it is easy to make the mistaken assumption that a Jewish congregation should avoid embracing the sinner. Yet, the galbanum teaches us otherwise. In order for a Jewish kehillah to be complete, it must embrace even the *poshim*, the sinners. While on an individual level one has to exercise extreme caution, on a communal level the kehillah is more effective when it is an amalgam of all kinds. Rav Yosef B. Soloveitchik, *zt"l*, states that the Hebrew word "*tzom*," meaning fast day, is related to the word "*tzama*," which means a braid. This

> The kehillah is more effective when it is an amalgam of all kinds of Jews.

indicates that the fast day is most potent when it contains the different strands of B'nei Yisrael.

Why is it that a congregation is more powerful when it includes wicked representatives? The *Prisha* suggests that the very fact that the wicked come to shul and make even a meager attempt at spirituality is a merit for the congregation. The *Drashos HaRan* states that their presence acts as an incentive for the righteous to pray on their behalf.

It is important for the pious majority of a congregation to be *m'karev* wayward people rather than taking the more common position of "How can we get rid of these people and be free of their company?" In our day and age where shuls grow precipitously, it invariably creates breakaways and fragments. We need to ask ourselves if we are learning the lesson of the *chelbenah*, the vital ingredient of galbanum in Hashem's *k'tores*.

May we embrace this complex lesson of tolerance and caring, and learn to balance the mitzvos of personally staying away from harmful influences while embracing the *poshei Yisrael* in the context of the community. In that merit, may Hashem always listen to our prayers and bless us with true peace.

Why Do Some Prayers Go Unanswered?

As Jews, we are taught that when we need something, we should pray to Hashem for His assistance. However, what do we do when we have prayed our hardest – and it doesn't seem as if our prayers have been accepted? Why is it that sometimes our prayers seem ineffective? There are many possible reasons for this troubling phenomenon.

First, there are times when our mouths are unable to be the proper vehicle to suitably convey our requests to Hashem. If, God forbid, we habitually yell at our spouses and co-workers, regularly speak *lashon hara* or use foul language, this deadens the power of our speech. As we are taught, "*Ein kateigor na'aseh saneigor*—The prosecutor cannot also be the defender." Thus, if we sully our speech with gossip about others, telling lies, revealing secrets or engaging in quarrels, we lose our power to successfully petition Hashem with tefillah. It is for this reason that the *metzora*, the biblical leper, has to cry out to passersby, "*Tameh, tameh*—I am contaminated, I am contaminated." This is not simply to alert people to keep their distance from him, but rather it is also a plea that others should pray for him, since the *metzora*—who is a

> If we sully our speech with gossip, lies or quarrels, we lose our power to successfully petition Hashem with tefillah.

"motzi ra" (one who speaks evil about others)—has lost the power to pray effectively for himself.

Another reason why our prayers are sometimes not helpful is because we don't put enough kavanah into our requests. It's helpful to remember the words of the *Chovos Halevavos*: Prayer without kavanah is like a body without a soul. Now, a body without a soul is otherwise known as a corpse. So, to be blunt, prayers without proper thought are prayers that really belong in the morgue! It is no wonder that such prayers will often be ineffective.

Sometimes, when we don't see results from our prayers, it may be because, unknown to us, there is a specified amount of prayer that Hashem expects from us for our particular need. We find that Moshe Rabbeinu prayed 515 prayers to Hashem to enter into Eretz Yisrael. The Midrash knows this since the gematria of *v'eschanan* (the description of Moshe's beseeching) equals 515. Similarly, we find that our mother Leah prayed so hard to be spared from becoming the wife of Eisav that her eyelashes fell out. In the same vein, the Gemara asks why our matriarchs were barren and answers, *"Mipnei sheHakadosh Baruch Hu misaveh l'tefilasan*—For Hashem desired their many prayers" (*Yevamos* 64a).

In this area, our relationship with Hashem differs from our relationship with our fellow man. In dealing with others, we might ask for something once—or maybe even twice. After that, if we ask a third time, we run the risk of being consider a pest. By the fifth time, our friends will seriously consider getting an unlisted number. However, when it comes to Hashem, we are taught to ask, and ask, and ask again. Indeed, the Gemara wonders what a person should do if he prays and his prayers go unanswered. The Gemara in *Brachos* (32b) advises, "*Yachzor v'yispallel*—Pray again," citing the verse, "*Kavei el Hashem, chazak v'yaameitz libecha, v'kavei el Hashem*—Hope to Hashem, take courage, be strong of heart, and hope to Hashem again." So don't be daunted if your prayers so far are unheeded. Redouble your efforts and keep on praying.

Sometimes, our prayers are successful and they create a *shefa bracha*, a flow of blessing. However, we might not see any results yet because we haven't made the proper hishtadlus. Perhaps, indeed, Hashem has the shidduch we need waiting for us, or a job right around the corner. We just need to make the effort to go out and find what we have prayed so hard for.

Finally, there are times that Hashem hears our prayers, but His answer is "No." We might be lacking sufficient merits or perhaps the result that we are praying for is not really in our best interests after all.

The Gemara in *Maseches Kala Rabasi* (chapter 3) suggests an effective method to help our prayers become more effective. The gematria of "*shalom*," 126, is the same gematria as "*shavei'a*" (to cry out). Thus, says the Gemara, "One who seeks peace will have his prayers answered." Help bring peace to your friends, neighbors and relations. The more we assume the role of a peacemaker, the more potent our prayers become.

May we be *zocheh* to pray effectively and for the right things. May Hashem accept and fulfill our prayers for our ultimate good.

Tefillah – Our Best Line of Defense

Let's zoom in on our greatest line of defense against harsh judgment—tefillah.

Let's examine what real tefillah is.

The Rambam teaches us that the *mitzvas asei* of prayer is derived from the verse, *"V'avad'tem es Hashem Elokeichem—You should serve Hashem your God"* (Shemos 23:25). How do we know that the verse is referring to the service of prayer? Maybe it means to serve Hashem by doing any one of the other numerous mitzvos. The answer is found in another verse where the Torah says, *"Ul'avdo bechol l'vavchem—To serve Him with all your heart"* (Devarim 11:13). On this pasuk, the Gemara expounds, *"Eizehu avoda shehi b'leiv? Hevei omer zu tefillah—What constitutes the service of the heart? The answer is prayer."* Thus, the Rambam concludes that when the Torah mandates "serving Hashem" without further explanation, it means to pray to Him.

If we analyze this commandment of prayer carefully, we will discover a very fundamental principle: The essence of the command to pray to Hashem is not speech-based. Rather, it revolves primarily around the arena of the heart. One of the major sources for many of the laws of prayer can be found in the verses in the Navi describing the eloquent prayers of Chanah. There it says, *"V'Chanah hi m'daberes al liba—And Chanah spoke with her heart"* (Shmuel I 1:13). This emphasizes that the heart is the vehicle of prayer.

The Zohar in Parshas Pekudei speaks very sternly about those who come to shul and only give lip service to Hashem, while their minds are far away. The Zohar says that the penalty for this very poor behavior is very great. Many people pride themselves on coming to shul, not talking and being careful to say every word of the tefillah. Perhaps, they even daven with grammatical accuracy. Sadly, they don't realize that if they don't concentrate on the meaning of the words and that they are talking to Hashem, they miss out on the very essence of the commandment.

Here's a further insight. The aforementioned Gemara says that the service of the heart is prayer. What exactly is the definition of this service? The ancient *Sefer HaEshkol* explains it as follows: The avodah of the heart is to strip away all worldly distractions when we come to pray to Hashem and to subjugate the heart, to concentrate on the prayers. Many of the early Chassidic masters have elaborated that the primary duty is the first component, to free the mind of all other mundane thoughts. As a reward for this service, Hashem will help us have proper kavanah.

We know that the Gemara in *Brachos* teaches, "*Tefillos k'neged korbanos tiknum*—The prayers were established to correspond to the sacrifices." Rav Shimon Schwab, zt"l, in his sefer on tefillah, discusses the fact that one of the steps of the service of korbanos in the Beis Hamikdash was *hefshet* (to skin the animal). The parallel service to this in our prayers is to shear away all our daily concerns and contemplations, such as what's waiting for us in the office, our plans for the weekend, what we're going to wear or eat and countless other distractions. We must cut away these extraneous thoughts and concentrate solely on heartfelt communication with Hashem.

Especially at this time of the year, when our prayer takes on a special tone of urgency and we petition Hashem for our health and well-being, let's work on this preparatory step of purging our hearts and minds of everything else and concentrate exclusively on the rarified privilege of praising and talking to the King of kings.

Emulating Hashem's Compassion

As the Yamim Noraim approach, we strive, through deep introspection, to see where we have erred, where we stand and how we are to approach Hashem. Often, because of our sins, we cannot approach from a position of strength. We have sinned and we can't make any excuses. The only practical solution seems to be to petition Hashem to judge us favorably in the name of His abundant mercy. We might not feel that we are deserving, but we can always ask for mercy.

Before Moshe Rabbeinu died, he begged Hashem to let him enter Eretz Yisrael. What type of tefillah did Moshe use? The Midrash tells us that there are ten different methods of prayer a person can utilize. In this instance, Moshe chose the method of "va'eschanan" ("he entreated"). Moshe did not ask Hashem to grant his request because of his merits. Nor did Moshe complain to Hashem. Moshe's form of prayer was derived from the language of "chein," which denotes the idea of getting something for free ("chinam"), solely due to Hashem's mercy. The Matnas Kehunah tells us that this is the best possible way to pray.

However, utilizing this mode of prayer comes with a price. If there was no price tag attached, then any sinner could just beg for Hashem's mercy and be forgiven. In *Maseches Shabbos* (15la), the Gemara specifies the criteria needed in order to daven for *rachamim*, mercy. "*Kol ha'm'rachaim al habrios, m'rachamim alav min hashamayim*—

> If we are compassionate to others, Hashem will be compassionate to us.

Whoever has mercy on others, God will have mercy on him." We must be compassionate toward others and Hashem will be compassionate toward us. So it is crucial that we prepare ourselves before we pray in this manner, to make sure we have the ammunition we need on the Yom HaDin.

When B'nei Yisrael committed the sin of the Golden Calf, Hashem taught Moshe a most powerful tefillah—the tefillah containing the Thirteen Middos of *Rachamim*. Hashem then told Moshe that whenever Klal Yisrael would cry out to Him with this tefillah, He would listen. In this tefillah, when we say "*Keil Rachum V'chanun*," we declare our belief in Hashem's abundant mercy. At the same time, this very same proclamation can work to our detriment. The Torah commands us, "*V'halachta bid'rachav*—Follow in His ways" (Devarim 28:9). We say in Az Yashir, "*Zeh Keili v'anveihu*—This is my God and I will glorify him" (Shemos 15:2). The Midrash tells us that "*anveihu*" is a contraction of two words, *ani* and *Hu* (I and Him). I will glorify Him by trying to be like Him. Looking at these two verses together, we learn to emulate Hashem by copying His middos (attributes). Consequently, if we pronounce the Thirteen Middos of *Rachamim* but we don't embody them as we are commanded to, it could very well work against us. Can't you just hear the prosecuting angel address the Holy Tribunal, "Listen to that person! He is begging for Hashem's mercy. He is admitting that Hashem is full of *rachamim*, but his own actions are far from merciful! On what grounds does he deserve Hashem's mercy?" This is why we have to truly arm ourselves with *rachmanus*, compassion toward others.

An example of a true *rachaman* was R' Shmuel Salant, who used to receive people in need at all hours of the day and night. As the years passed, his family saw the physical toll that this was taking on him, and wanted to limit his appointments to certain hours of the day. However, R' Shmuel refused, citing Birchas HaMazon, *"Um' farneis osanu tamid b'chol yom, u'v'chol eis, u'v'chol shaah*—Hashem supports us always, every day, every time, at every hour." Hashem is always on call, R' Shmuel protested, and we are supposed to emulate Him. Since Hashem is always available, R' Shmuel felt that he had to always be available as well.

The degree to which we behave with mercifulness toward others has a bearing on the effectiveness of our tefillos. In Devarim (33:12), the pasuk tells us, *"L'Binyamin amar: Y'did Hashem, yishcon lavetach alav*—To Binyamin [Moshe] said: Friend of Hashem, Hashem will dwell in security in his portion." Rashi explains that this refers to the fact that the Beis Hamikdash would be built in the portion of Binyamin. The *Yalkut Shimoni* explains why the tribe of Binyamin was chosen for this unique honor. For all the years of its existence, people would come to the Beis Hamikdash to daven to Hashem and beg for mercy. In order for their prayers to be effective, the Beis Hamikdash needed to be a place of compassion. Hashem, therefore, selected the portion of Binyamin, the most merciful of the twelve brothers, since he was the only one not involved in the cruel act of selling Yosef.

In short, the more merciful one is to others, the more merciful Hashem will be to him. If we concentrate on strengthening ourselves in the middah of *rachamim*, we can have confidence that Hashem will show mercy to us.

Hashem has given us a number of practical mitzvos to kindle, awaken and develop the priceless attribute of *rachmanus* within us. Hashem, Who desires only what is best for us, wants to help us in developing this essential trait. In order to do this, He gave us mitzvos that enhance feelings of empathy within us and help us feel compassion for others. One such mitzvah we have is *shiluach hakan*. We send away the mother bird before taking her eggs or her offspring so she is not there to witness her children being taken from her. The *K'sav Sofer* stresses the importance of this mitzvah as an act of mercy. It is a drill, an exercise, to help us feel the suffering of another. The Gemara (*Pesachim* 13b) tells us that if we are sensitive to the suffering and feeling of others, we will merit the blessing of "*L'maan yitav lach v'haarachta yamim—*so that it will be good for you and your days will be lengthened" (Devarim 22:7).

The Torah tells us: "*V'nasati eisev b'sadcha livhemtecha, v'achalta v'savata—*Hashem will give you grass in the fields for your animals, and you will eat and be satisfied" (Devarim 11:15). The Gemara (*Brachos* 40) explains that the Torah is telling us that we must feed our animals before we feed ourselves. The *mefarshim* further explain that this pasuk speaks to us not only about animals, but also about all those who are unable to help themselves. Before we sit down to breakfast, for example, we should make sure that all our children have food, that the baby has a bottle or that an elderly person in our care has eaten.

Unfortunately, we often do the right things, but for the wrong reasons. When our child cries in the middle of the night, we get up, change the baby's diaper and give her a bottle. Why do we do it? Because we want to be able to go back to sleep as quickly as possible? Because we don't want the neighbors to think we don't tend to our children? In truth, we should be doing it for one reason only—the child is uncomfortable and is suffering. We should feel that discomfort and rush to ease and soothe the child's pain. This is the level we must all aspire to—the great principle of the Torah, "*V'ahavta la'reiacha kamocha*—Love your brother as you do yourself" (Vayikra 19:18).

The root letters of *rachamim*—Reish, Ches and Mem—correspond to the *ramach aivarim*, the 248 limbs in a man's body. If one behaves mercifully, Hashem will be merciful in return and save one from bodily harm. Those letters are also the same as the letters in the word "*rechem*," meaning womb. There is no other place where the care for another human being is so complete and fundamental. An unborn child is totally dependent on its mother, and she supplies its every need. The same letters also comprise the word "*chamor*" (donkey). A donkey goes through life carrying people's burdens. A person who is merciful also carries the burdens of others. What of someone who does not care at all for anyone besides himself? For such a heartless individual, the root letters of *rachamim* can also be rearranged to spell *"cheirem"* (expulsion).

The Gemara illustrates just how dangerous it is to cause pain to another person. It tells us how Avdan caused distress to R' Yishmael bar R' Yosi. Because of this, Avdan became a leper, two of his sons died and two other sons suffered divorce from their wives. The Gemara in *Kesuvos* (62b) tells us of R' Rechumi, who was a student of Rava in Mechuza. He learned there all year round and only came home once a year, on Erev Yom Kippur. One year, however, he was so engrossed in learning that he forgot to go home. His wife, who was eagerly awaiting her husband's return, started to cry when he did not appear. As her tears flowed, the roof that her husband was learning on collapsed, and he was killed.

A person has to feel *rachmanus* for all Jews, but it is especially important that we feel compassion for our spouses. We are not on guard when we are with them. We usually feel that we don't have to impress them. We subconsciously rely on the fact that they are stuck with us regardless of our behavior. At the same time, our tolerance for their mistakes is very low, especially when they repeat the same offense more than once. But despite all this, we have to be very careful. Hurting your spouse could be deadly!

Another famous example of the consequences of insensitivity to others is found in the book of Shmuel Aleph (chapter 1). Penina taunted Chana relentlessly about her childlessness, but only so that Chana would turn to Hashem and pray more fervently for a child. Her intentions were l'sheim shamayim (for a good purpose). However, because of the suffering she caused, all of her children died tragically in her lifetime. Hurting someone is like putting your hand in a fire. No matter why you put your hand in it, no matter how good the excuse, you cannot come away unscathed.

> Hurting someone is like putting your hand in a fire. No matter why you put your hand in it, you cannot come away unscathed.

The *Yerushalmi Pe'ah* (3:1) tells us of R' Pinchas ben Yair and his talmidim. They were traveling on a road when a flash flood hit, creating an impassable river that barred their way. R' Pinchas called out to the river to let him pass. The river split, and R' Pinchas crossed to the other side. His talmidim called to him and asked that he make the river split for them as well. R' Pinchas replied that whoever had never hurt another person in their entire lives could approach the river and it would part.

We must all work on ourselves to develop the sensitivity we need to be merciful and compassionate to our spouses, to our children and to every Yid in Klal Yisrael. When we ask Hashem for His mercy, we want Him to see that we have tried to emulate his ways and are true *baalei rachamim*. In the merit of our increased sensitivity to others, may Hashem bless us all with His infinite *rachamim*.

Rosh Hashanah: Heeding the Shofar's Blast

We say in Selichos, *"K'dalim uch'rashim, dafaknu d'lasecha*—Like the needy and the poor, we bang on Your door." This statement seems to be a paradox. When a person is needy and destitute, he is usually meek and timid. It's not likely that he would be banging on anyone's door. The commentators explain that when one is desperate enough, he bangs, even if he is embarrassed. Thus, the person who has not eaten for five days will pound on the door for food, no matter how timid he is. So, too, although we realize that we are poor in deeds and weak in Torah, we are also aware that, as the Day of Judgment nears, we are desperate. We are not ashamed to knock loudly on Hashem's doors of mercy.

The pasuk says, *"K'nesher ya'ir kino*—Like the eagle who awakens her nest" (Devarim 32:11). Rashi explains that the eagle does not swoop down suddenly upon her nest, for if she would do so, she would severely startle her young. Instead, she rustles the neighboring branches with her wings to alert them that she is on the way. So, too, Hashem in His kindness does not suddenly spring the Yom HaDin upon us. Instead, metaphorically, He "rustles the branches" during the month of Elul, giving us a chance to prepare properly for the day of reckoning. The rustling branches are the sound of the shofar blast every morning. The Rambam teaches us that the shofar's message is: *"Uru yesheinim m'sheinaschem*—Awaken, you sleepers from your slumber." The shofar heralds the urgent message that we must prepare wisely for the critical day of Rosh Hashanah.

There are other significant messages of the shofar. The *K'sav Sofer* says that the word "shofar" reminds us, "*Shapru* (consisting of the same letters as shofar) *ma'aseichem*— Improve and beautify your deeds." The shofar is reminding us that throughout the month, we should analyze our good deeds and try to make them even better. The *K'sav Sofer* also advises us that the correct order of business during Elul is, "*Sur meira va'asei tov*—Turn away from evil and do good" (Tehillim 34:46). Thus, we must first concentrate on removing the bad from within us. This includes anger, foul speech, destructive gossip, gazing at forbidden things, laxity in kashrus and so forth.

> We know we are succeeding in life when we manage to break our natural sinful tendencies.

The Gemara in *Rosh Hashanah* teaches us that we specifically use the horn of a ram as a shofar because it is bent. This reminds us of one of the most important callings of life: to bend our evil inclination to the service of Hashem. We know we are succeeding in life when we manage to break our natural sinful tendencies. When we awaken with alacrity for prayer or study, we "bend" away from our tendency toward laziness. When we give tzedaka or a loan, we thereby overcome our natural selfishness. When we hold back a biting, sarcastic reply, help out even when we are tired and have patience for our children and spouses, we have succeeded in "bending" away from the calls of our Yetzer Hara.

Rav Zev Leff, *shlit"a*, shared a fascinating insight with me about the message of the shofar. He points out that the shofar can never go up on the *mizbeyach*, nor can it be eaten with religious intent. The Kohanim and those bringing the korban eat other parts of the sacrifices. This part of the animal has no religious significance other than as a shofar. Yet, on Rosh Hashanah, the shofar is catapulted into the forefront, becoming the centerpiece of our atonement process. Rav Leff explains that one of the defining points of the shofar is its location on the ram. The horns are situated above the head and they symbolize that which is beyond our understanding. In other words, since the shofar's place is above the brain, it represents the mitzvos that we do even though we cannot grasp the reasons for them. It highlights the mitzvos that we don't understand but do purely out of love and obedience for Hashem.

Perhaps this is why the pasuk says, *"Tiku bachodesh shofar ... ki chok l'Yisrael hu*—Blow, this month, the shofar ... for it is a statute for Yisrael" (Tehillim 81:4). *Chukim*, statutes, are the commandments of the Torah that we fulfill even though we don't understand them. We do them only to follow Hashem's will. Thus, we avoid wearing *shaatnez*, we don't mix meat and milk and we strive to fulfill all 613 mitzvos, even when we don't understand why.

This is one of the primary reminders of the shofar: Hashem is our Boss and we are committed to follow Him always—whether or not we understand. This is why, when we crown Hashem as our King on Rosh Hashanah, we do so through the vehicle of the shofar. How fitting that we pay homage to the King with a symbol of our dedication to always follow Him, even when His directives are above and beyond our understanding.

May we merit to follow the messages of the shofar: avoiding evil, improving ourselves, bending our inclinations to Hashem's ways and following Him at all times.

Yom Kippur: Tipping the Scales

When the chazzan intones, *"Mi yichyeh umi yamus—* Who will live and who (chas v'shalom) will die," we all quake in our boots, and rightly so. So what can we do to improve our chances for a positive judgment on Yom Kippur?

The Gemara tells us that Hashem initially creates every husband and wife as one. Indeed, forty days before a child's conception, a Bas Kol announces that child's bashert (*Sotah* 2a). So, in fact, we are preprogrammed to complement our spouses, and it is Hashem's desire that we should live out our lives together with our predestined match. Even if we are otherwise undeserving, if we fulfill our marital responsibilities, we give Hashem a strong reason to view us as indispensable. On the Day of Judgment, it is a powerful defense to pledge to Hashem that in the coming year we will try harder to make our spouse's life sweeter, happier and more fulfilled.

The Gemara informs us that Nadav and Avihu (the two saintly children of Aharon who passed away tragically during the dedication of the Mishkan) died because they were not married and didn't have children. This is rather mystifying. The Torah tells us explicitly that Nadav and Avihu died because they offered a "foreign fire" in the Mishkan, one that Hashem had not commanded them to bring. The commentaries explain this puzzle by acknowledging that it was true that their sin was bringing a foreign fire, but had they been married, having wives would have saved them from punishment. If they had had children, then those children would have saved them. Had they devoted themselves to a spouse and family, they would have been considered too valuable for Hashem to take them away.

This is the advice that the *Orchos Chaim* offers: "*Harotzeh l'ha'arich yamim, hevei marbeh b'achim v'rei'im*—If someone wants to live long, he should try to have many relatives and friends." Thus, we see that the more we make ourselves needed, the more secure our lives become. Even if we deserve to die, there are people in our lives who don't deserve the pain of our loss. Although Hashem has no lack of available helpers, no one can replace a biological father and mother, a loving child or an attentive and helpful spouse.

> The more we make ourselves needed, the more secure our lives become.

Therefore, a husband should carefully consider whether or not he is properly fulfilling his wife's needs. The Gemara (*Pesachim* 109a) informs us that clothing creates a special joy for a woman. The wise husband will be diligent in attending to his wife's happiness in this way. A wife should ask herself if she can improve in those areas where she alone can bring happiness to her husband, for in that way she makes herself truly indispensable and fulfills her very essential role of being an "*eizer k'negdo*." Indeed, during the Aseres Y'mei Teshuvah, spouses should ask each other not just for forgiveness, but also for concrete suggestions on how they can make each other happier in the coming year.

When it comes to our children, we should consider how to connect with them more frequently in spite of our fast-paced lives. We should make it our business to know each child's favorite nosh, which bedtime story is his favorite and what compliment especially warms his heart. To create a twinkle in a child's eye and to bring simcha to a child is a great mitzvah. We should try to make a commitment to Hashem that we will increase our efforts at trying to emulate Avraham Avinu by inculcating awareness of Hashem into our children.

When it comes to our parents, nothing beats visiting, calling and writing to them more often. They don't have to live in Eretz Yisrael for them to enjoy a letter from us. A postcard sent from Boro Park to Flatbush is just as touching and might be read and reread many times. Let's make a commitment to ensure that they are clothed properly for the winter, and that they have the appropriate food, medical attention and everything else they need.

Let's try to be there for our friends. Let's make a commitment that whenever we notice one of our acquaintances has taken sick, we will make sure to call. We know how much we appreciate a phone call when we are under the weather.

Let's make sure to tell Hashem: Hashem, we don't want anyone to be punished on our account. We don't want someone to be put into traction, lose his job or get depressed because they might have hurt or insulted us. So we forgive them before this holiest of Days. But let's make a deal. We are forgiving them even though they may not really deserve it. So You, Who reward measure for measure, should please forgive us for our many faults, even though we don't deserve

Rabbi Moshe Meir Weiss

it either. Burying the hatchet, overcoming grudges and abolishing feuds all create a setting conducive to a positive *middah k'neged middah*, measure for measure, result. We forgive others and Hashem will, in turn, forgive us and bury our misdeeds. As the Gemara teaches us, *"Kol hama'avir al midosav, ma'avirin lo al kol p'sha'av*—Whoever overlooks the ills that others do to him will have his sins overlooked" (*Yoma* 23a).

When we live with constant awareness of Hashem, it is Hashem's pleasure to keep us around for a long, long time. After all, as we say in the wedding blessing, *"Shehakol bara lichvodo*—He created everything for His honor." If we fit in with Hashem's plan, Hashem will allow us to remain here for a long while.

We know that *"M'zonosav shel adam k'tzuvin lo meiRosh Hashanah*—A person's livelihood is fixed for him on Rosh Hashanah" (*Beizah* 16b). Therefore, besides the obvious responsibility to pray fervently for a sufficient annual income, this is also the time to work on incorporating the attitude that our parnassa is from Hashem, and to embrace a lifestyle that embodies that outlook.

To illustrate what this means, let me share with you a beautiful parable from the Dubno Maggid. He tells the story of a pauper who is trudging along with a heavy backpack. A wealthy coachman drives by and offers him a ride. Gratefully, the pauper climbs in, but even though he is sitting, he keeps the heavy burden on his back. The driver asks in consternation, "Why are you still holding your heavy pack? Put it down." The poor man replies that it is enough that he is giving him a ride, he doesn't want to trouble the coachman with the burden of carrying the package, too. The coachman laughs and says, "Either way, it's in the coach. You might as well put it down and enjoy the ride."

The Dubno Maggid says that it is the same with one's efforts at making a living. Of course, we can't rest on our laurels. We can't sit back and just assume that whatever we are supposed to get will come along anyway. Rather, we must make the proper *hishtadlus* to get our annual stipend. Still, it is foolhardy to spend more time working than Hashem expects from us. If we work long hours, and as a result forego things like praying with a minyan, a fixed Torah learning session or studying with our children, then we know that we have taken *hishtadlus* too far. After all, Hashem is giving us a ride anyway. Why don't we put down our bags and trust in Him? As the pasuk says, *"Hashleich al Hashem y'havcha, v'hu yechalk'lecha*—Cast upon Hashem your burden and He will sustain you"* (Tehillim 55:23). So let's commit ourselves to spending more time with the family, more time in shul, more time learning and more time on chesed, and let's leave the extra hours of income for Hashem to take care of.

> Hashem is giving us a ride anyway. Why don't we put down our bags and trust in Him?

Let's be proactive when it comes to Yom Kippur: *"L'olam y'vakeish adam rachamim shelo yecheleh*—A person should always pray not to become sick"* (*Shabbos* 32a). Let's not take for granted any of our good fortune or Hashem's kindness. It is also a wonderful idea for people to pray for each other. This method of tefillah is precious in Hashem's eyes. As we are taught, *"Kol hamivakeish rachamim al chaveiro, v'hu* *tzarich la'oso davar, hu ne'eneh techilah*—Whoever asks for mercy on behalf of his friend when he shares the same need will have his own prayers answered first" (*Bava Kama* 92a).

In fact, I try to make it a point to pray for the health and well-being of my wonderful readership—for those who need a cure, for those who want children and for those who are seeking a mate. I try to have in mind all those who seek wisdom in dealing with their children, those who need employment and those who wish for increased marital bliss. For everyone seeking a new year of good health and prosperity—I am mispallel for you and it is my hope that all of you will find a few minutes to do the same for me.

The Gift of Tzedaka

Thus far, we have looked at two of the three ingredients that repeal any evil decrees—for as we say in the Rosh Hashanah and Yom Kippur liturgy, "*Teshuvah, tefillah, u'tzedaka ma'avirin es ro'ah ha-gezeirah*—Repentance, prayer and charity remove the evil of the decree." We've discussed repentance, and we've covered prayer. Now let's take a serious look at the third ingredient—tzedaka.

The pasuk teaches us that, "*Tzedaka tatzil mimaves*—Charity saves one from death" (Mishlei 10:2). This is particularly important when we pray for life on the Yom HaDin, the Day of Judgment. Since Rosh Hashanah is also the time when Hashem distributes our annual income, it behooves us to beef up on our tzedaka output, for the Torah promises us, "*Aser t'aser*—You shall surely give tithes" (Devarim 14:22)). The Gemara explains, "*Aser bishvil shetisasher*—Give tithes and you will become wealthy" (*Shabbos* 119a).

At this point, one might wonder, "Wait a minute! I know a lot of people who diligently give charity and are not wealthy! To the contrary, they are still struggling." This question is dealt with in several ways by a variety of commentators. The Chofetz Chaim explains that while a person might give charity, he doesn't get the Divine reward of wealth unless he gives in proportion to his means. Sometimes, when there is a Hatzalah appeal in shul, everyone, rich and poor alike, calls out one hundred dollars! This is not in the proper spirit of tzedaka. Everyone is supposed to give according to his means—and we all have different means. The Chofetz Chaim cites a frightening example of the consequences of holding back tzedaka. During the period leading up to the Churban Bayis Sheini, the Jews of Yerushalayim were besieged and starving. The daughter of Nakdimon ben Gurion was found picking barleycorns out of dung in order to survive. The Gemara asks how such a thing could have happened to the daughter of so great a philanthropist. The Gemara answers that, indeed, her father Nakdimon gave a lot of charity—but not according to his ability.

Furthermore, the Marchazu tells us that one isn't rewarded with wealth unless one gives his charity happily. The Torah says, "*V'lo yeirah levavcha b'sitcha lo*—Let not your heart be pained when you give of your money to the poor" (Devarim 15:10). This is, indeed, a great challenge

> Everyone is supposed to give according to his means—and we all have different means.

for many people. Although we give tzedaka, when people knock on the door, call on the phone or ask us in shul, we often give it grudgingly or with a frown. In order to receive Divine reward, we need to train ourselves to give tzedaka with a smile.

My favorite answer to the question of why those who give charity are not always rewarded with wealth is explained by the *Hafla'ah*. He explains that the blessings of wealth for giving charity are not apparent in one's bankbook. He quotes the Gemara that says that the reward for giving tzedaka is *"shetisasher,"* that one will become *"asher"* (wealthy). The Mishnah in *Pirkei Avos* says, *"Eizehu ashir? Hasamei'ach b'chelko*—Who is wealthy? He who is satisfied with his lot."* The *Hafla'ah* concludes

> The reward of charity is a sense of satisfaction and well-being.

that the reward of charity is a sense of satisfaction and well-being. This is indeed the prophecy in Malachi (3:10)—that for giving charity, Hashem will open up the skylight in Heaven: *"V'harikosi lachem bracha ad bli dai,"* which the Gemara explains to mean that Hashem will shower reward upon the Baal Tzedaka until his lips will tire from saying *"enough!"* This, the *Hafla'ah* says, is a poetic way of expressing an attitude of fulfillment and well-being.

I believe that one of the reasons why the Torah offers so many wonderful "lollipops" for the philanthropic person is because there is a stern Torah directive on how to give charity. The Torah demands from us, *"V'lo yeirah levavcha b'sitcha lo*—Let not your heart be pained when you give of your money to the poor."* Now, this is understandably a very tough commandment to uphold, especially if one lives on a tight budget. It is not easy to part with your hard-earned money without feeling a natural pang of dismay. Therefore, Hashem offers all of these luscious rewards to assure us that when we take money out of our wallet to give to the poor, we are not losing anything even in this world. Rather, we are making one of the most prudent investments available to mankind.

Of course, when it comes to our Rosh Hashanah

preparations, we are especially interested in the assurance that *"Tzedaka tatzil mimaves,"* for, as we know, on Yom Kippur, the Book of Life and the Book of Death are open before Hashem and He renders the final seal of our fates for each and every one of us on this awesome day.

Why is it that charity is unique in its ability to save our lives? Why don't we say *"Shabbos tatzil mimaves,"* or *"Kashrus tatzil mimaves"* or perhaps *"Taharas hamishpacha tatzil mimaves"*? What is so special about charity that it is vested with such awesome power?

Let's explain with a practical example. You make $25 per hour at work. You go to shul on Shabbos and they have an appeal for Hatzalah, the local Bikur Cholim or your community yeshiva or day school. You benevolently respond by pledging $100. In essence, what are you giving to charity? It took you four hours to earn that money, so what you are really doing is giving four hours of your life to charity. We know that Hashem rewards in a very liberal way, measure-for-measure, for the mitzvos that we do. Therefore, since we are giving a portion of our life to charity, Hashem will reward us with extra life. Charity literally saves us from death.

The Chida, *zt"l*, comments on the repetitive phrasing used in the pasuk: *"Nason titein v'lo yeirah levovcha b'sitcha lo ki biglal hadavar hazeh yivarechecha Hashem Elokecha*—You should surely give to the poor and it should not hurt you to give to him, because for the sake of this mitzvah Hashem your God will bless you." He explains that one of the most powerful ways to give tzedaka is *matan b'seiser,* giving in secret. Even if Hashem is, *chas v'shalom,* angry at us, the pasuk in Mishlei (21:14) teaches us, *"Matan b'seiser yichpei af—*

A gift in secret pacifies anger." Giving charity in secret squelches the Divine wrath.

Pure *matan b'seiser* is when the giver doesn't know to whom he is giving and the poor man doesn't know from whom he is receiving. Too often nowadays, people give charity but expect something in return. They want a say in how the yeshiva is run or in what direction a shul should take, or, if they are giving to the needy, they like the feeling that the people should be indebted to them. This is not the pure spirit of tzedaka. The Chida explains that the pasuk says "*nason titein*" to allude to the fact that there should be two separate givings. First, the one who gives the charity should give it to a *gabbai tzedaka*, a charity collector. Then, the charity collector should distribute it to the poor. This is true *matan b'seiser*.

The Chida offers another explanation for the repetitive "*nason titein*." He cites the famous question of the Rambam. If one has a hundred dollars for tzedaka, what is the proper way to distribute it? Should he give it all to one poor person or should he give one dollar apiece to one hundred poor people? One might reason that it's better to give a hundred-dollar bill to one person and make a meaningful impact, but the Rambam decides to the contrary. He explains that it's better to give one dollar to a hundred people. Instead of doing one *maiseh mitzvah*, one mitzvah action, he is doing one hundred of them. Instead of overcoming his Yetzer Hara once, he is conquering it one hundred times. This, explains the Chida, is another reason why it says "*nason titein*"—to allude to the fact that one should make sure to do multiple givings.

On Pesach, we wear a kittel to the Seder. When it comes

time to hustle the afikomen away from the prying hands of children and grandchildren (and an occasional spouse), the head of the house looks in vain for a pocket in his kittel to stash that precious piece of matzah. In exasperation, he says to himself, "Why don't they put pockets in these things?" The reason why the kittel has no pockets is because it is the Jewish *tachrichin* (burial shrouds) in which we are buried after 120 years. It deliberately has no pockets to teach us a vital lesson. When we die, we cannot take anything material with us on our final Heavenly journey—not even our Titanium American Express card! As the verse expresses so eloquently, "*Lo b'moso yikach hakol*—For in death we don't take anything with us," and as the Tanna teaches us, "*Ein m'lavin l'adam b'shaas moso ela mitzvos u'ma'asim tovim bilvad*—All that escorts a person on his final journey is his fulfillment of the Torah and acts of kindness."

I heard an interesting observation from Rav Berel Wein, *shlit"a*. He pointed out that Sir Moses Montifiore has more hospitals, schools and charitable organizations named for him than any other Jew in history. Montifiore was a generous man, a philanthropist of global proportions. Legend has it that in his mansion, Sir Moses had a room that contained only a simple, empty coffin. Every night before retiring, he would lie down in this coffin for a few moments. It helped him remember that, one day, this would be all that he would have left from his vast worldly possessions.

In America, we are used to measuring our success by the size of our investment portfolio, by the collection of our assets and our expensive toys and gadgets. However, this wealth is only temporary. Unfortunately, in the course of my

Rabbanus, I have given hundreds of eulogies. I have never eulogized a person by saying how vast his assets were or how shrewd his investments were. If the person was a giving and sharing individual, that was the headline news at his funeral.

It is imperative that we train ourselves to prioritize how we spend our money. Then, after carving out a significant slice of our annual budget for tzedaka, we should try to take it to the next level. We have to feel happy and accomplished about the ways we give. We need to start a portfolio for the Afterlife. In this portfolio, we can keep a daily record of what we invest for the next world: the Torah we learned, the prayers said with the right kavanah, the actions that made our spouse happy, quality time we spent with the children or moments devoted to honoring and caring for our parents. Our tzedaka can be permanently recorded in this portfolio. As we say in our davening, *"Zoreiah tzedakos"*—when we give charity, we are "planting" our tzedaka. Such a daily drill will cause us to realize that when we write out a check to a poor person, Torah institution or other needy charity, we are not giving our money away. We aren't losing something we've worked hard for. Rather, we are investing permanently and securely—with no chance of loss—in our own eternity.

We must remember that the Gemara says in *Bava Basra* (10b) that Hashem gives us a certain amount of money that is supposed to be given for tzedaka. If we don't use it properly and wisely, Hashem will take it away from us

> We need to start a portfolio for the Afterlife, where we keep a daily record of what we invest for the next world.

anyway. It might go to the tax collector, a rent increase or a broken water boiler, but we won't benefit from it. Ultimately, we'll have lost both the money and the great rewards that we could have received from giving it to tzedaka—both in this world and in the next.

May it be the will of Hashem that we learn to invest wisely, the Jewish way, and in this merit may Hashem bless us with good health, happiness and the satisfaction of doing the right thing.

Keeping Our Commitments

Sukkos is finally here! As we sit in the shade of our beautiful sukkah, we can reflect on the challenging period of Elul and the High Holy Days that have just passed. A lot of time and effort has been spent in trying to improve our lives and in communicating with Hashem. As Yom Kippur neared, we made commitments in a variety of areas. We pledged to find more time for Torah study, and we promised to concentrate more on our prayers and be more serious about our brachos. We resolutely decided to devote more time to our marriages and to our children. We determined to be more careful with our speech and planned to be much more scrupulous with giving charity.

Now, the fear of the Day of Judgment is behind us— and the reminders of the shofar, HaMelech Hakadosh, and Avinu Malkeinu have passed. Now we need to gird ourselves to the real challenge, that of keeping to our commitments.

This is reminiscent of the situation facing one who mourns a close relative. During the days of shiva, he is flooded by a veritable barrage of friends and relatives coming to comfort him. He is supported by family and community. The real challenge of coping with loss is after the shiva period, when everyone leaves and the mourner is

> The true test of our teshuvah is when we go home and face our everyday challenges alone.

alone to face his grief. Similarly, on Yom Kippur, while everyone around us is *"clopping"* his chest and saying the Viduy with contrition, it is easy to get caught up in the spirit of teshuvah. The true test, however, is when we go home and face our everyday challenges alone. This is the acid test of determining how committed we really are.

The Gemara in *Maseches Yoma* (86b) teaches us that if one does teshuvah out of fear of retribution, he converts his willful sins into unwitting transgressions. This is certainly a nifty trick. However, there is an even better possibility! The Gemara continues that if one does teshuvah *mei'ahava*, because of his love for Hashem, then *"z'donos na'asos lo kiz'chuyos—* willful sins are converted into *merits."* This is a remarkable boon from Hashem. One's misdeeds can actually be changed into mitzvos. The *Shai LaTorah* explains this unique phenomenon as follows: The mitzvah of teshuvah, which is one of the 613 mitzvos, would not be possible without sin. So, if a person does a wholesome teshuvah, it turns out that this sin is a *hechsher mitzvah*—a preparatory act for the fulfillment of the mitzvah of teshuvah, and there is a Talmudic adage that *"hechsher mitzvah k'mitzvah*—the preparatory act of a mitzvah is like the mitzvah itself." It is for this reason that eating on Erev Yom Kippur is considered as important as fasting. Since the eating enables us to be better prepared for the fast, it is a *hechsher mitzvah* and thus like the mitzvah itself. So, the unique result is that the eating is as if one is fasting! So, too, when one does teshuvah out of love, his sin indeed becomes a component of the mitzvah itself.

Rav Boruch Ber, *zt"l*, wonders why there is such a vast difference between one who does teshuvah out of fear and one who does teshuvah out of love. He gives a beautiful explanation. When one repents because of fear of Divine punishment, he does not necessarily regret his transgressions. He just exercises repentance out of fear of the sin's repercussions. However, when one does teshuvah because of his love for Hashem, then he regrets the actual sin. He is full of remorse for going against the will of his beloved Creator. It is this type of teshuvah that can convert a sin into an actual mitzvah.

If we understand that the loftiest teshuvah is teshuvah done out of love, we can appreciate that it is only after Yom Kippur when we can really first roll up our sleeves and get to work. During the High Holy Days, our motivation is primarily out of fear of judgment and Hashem's verdict. Now, when the Judgment Day has passed and we are sitting in our sukkos, basking in the nostalgic memories of Hashem's loving protection, we can focus on the purest form of teshuvah. We can repent out of our deep love for Hashem, Who has chosen us and given us so many things in this world and a glorious future in the Eternity.

We have a very pleasant outcome to look forward to. As we repent with love, we can convert our past mistakes and misdeeds into lofty mitzvos. So, instead of being burdened with guilt, let's get cracking at this lofty mission. May it be the will of Hashem that we succeed with a teshuvah sheleima, a perfect repentance in all areas of life.

Hoshanah Rabbah
Wake-up Call

207

Hoshanah Rabbah is a special and unique day. Our tradition teaches us that on Hoshanah Rabbah, the verdicts of Rosh Hashanah and Yom Kippur are given to angelic messengers for final execution. As such, it is a final day of appeal. It's our last chance to overturn any possible bad decree, *chas v'shalom.*

Did you ever wonder why Hashem constructed the Jewish calendar in such a way that the Ten Days of Repentance come right after Rosh Hashanah, the Day of Judgment? Why didn't Hashem make a day of petitioning and contrition before Rosh Hashanah? It makes more sense to prepare ourselves before the big day. Perhaps we can glean an understanding about this by looking at a practical comparison. Did you ever notice the way some young people take exams? For weeks before a big test is scheduled they do practically nothing. Then, the day before the test they cram feverishly, studying around the clock. They take the exam, get a passing grade and the next day they've forgotten everything they've studied.

> Hashem doesn't want us to "cram" our repentance the way some people do for final exams.

Hashem did not want this to be the situation with our New Year's commitments. He didn't want the fear of

Hoshanah Rabbah Wake-up Call

judgment at year's end to force us to "cram" our repentance. We would make all sorts of last-minute desperate promises and commitments, only to see them fall by the wayside at the very beginning of the New Year. So Hashem in His mercy placed the Aseres Y'mei Teshuvah, the Ten Days of Repentance, after Rosh Hashanah so that we can demonstrate to Hashem that we are starting off the year on the right foot.

Then, after the festive holiday of Sukkos, at the close of the Yom Tov, Hashem gives us the awesome day of Hoshanah Rabbah. It's a day on which we can check our spiritual pulses and see whether we are keeping up with our New Year's resolutions. Are we keeping our promises to be gentler to our spouse and more attentive to our friends? Are we finding more time for our children and more time for our learning? Are we keeping to our regimen of davening more slowly and with more kavanah?

We pray to Hashem that He deliver us only good verdicts, and that He should help us bring all our positive resolutions to fruition. In the merit of all our struggles, may we be blessed with only good.

In loving memory of
a dear talmid and good friend

יקותיאל יהודה בן יעקב נחמיה ז״ל

George Hersko

ת.נ.צ.ב.ה.

Dedicated by

Rabbi and Mrs. Moshe Meir Weiss,
by his loving wife Beverly
and children Shara, Jenny, and Adam,
and by his good friends,
Chaim Pretter, Les Abrahams,
Motty Eisenberger and Mark Rosenblum

Dedicated in loving memory of

Avrohom Ben Nissim Gordon, ז״ל

May the merit of those learning this sefer
help those that are in need of a shidduch
find their life's mate quickly and easily,
and all those that desire children be
blessed speedily with healthy offspring.

by

Mr. Richard and Frima Gordon

לע״נ

רב דוד בן יוסף יונה צבי הלוי הורוביץ

לע״נ

הינדא לאה חיה בת רב אברהם גרינוואלד

and with much *hakaras hatov*
for the Torah and *chesed* of
Rabbi Moshe Meir Weiss
and Miriam Libby Weiss, שליט״א

Dedicated by

Yehuda and Shiffy Greenwald

In loving memory of

Julius and Greta Pfeiffer, ז״ל

and Max Goldberg, ז״ל

ת.נ.צ.ב.ה.

Dedicated by

Milton and Fran Pfeiffer

לז״נ
אהרן בן יעקב שלום
לאה בת בנימן
שווארץ

לזכרון עולם בהיכל ה'

מוקדש לזכר ולעילוי נשמת האשה החשובה

יהודית סערקע בת ר' יצחק אייזיק גאלדבערג ע"ה

נפטרה י"ט שבט תשנ"ד

מאת בניה ונכדיה שיחי'

ר' יצחק בן ציון ורחל גאלדה קורצער

אהרן, חיה שרה, קלמן אברהם, איטא מלכה,

שמואל מנחם, יהודית סערקע, משה נח,

שמואל זאב, לאה פייגא

May the learning from this sefer
also be a zechus for my father

ר' אהרן צבי בן ר' מאיר וייס זצ"ל

Mr. Heshy Weiss, *zt"l*

and for my wife's parents

ר' אהרן בן משה געלבטוך זצ"ל

ומ' דבורה בת ר' אריה לייב זצ"ל

Mr. Aaron & Devora Gelbtuch, *zt"l*

ת.נ.צ.ב.ה.

Dedicated by

Rabbi Moshe Meir & Miriam Libby Weiss

In loving memory of

משה בן שמואל יהודה ז״ל
רבקה בת שמואל פנחס ז״ל
ת.נ.צ.ב.ה.

יפה מלכה אסתר בת לאה
לאה בת בת שבע
לרפואה שלמה בתוך שאר חולי ישראל

from

The Roz Family

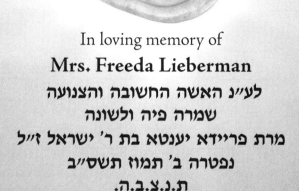

In loving memory of

Mrs. Freeda Lieberman

לע״נ האשה החשובה והצנועה
שמרה פיה ולשונה
מרת פריידא יענטא בת ר׳ ישראל ז״ל
נפטרה ב׳ תמוז תשס״ב
ת.נ.צ.ב.ה.

Dedicated by her loving mishpacha

Morris and Lily Lieberman

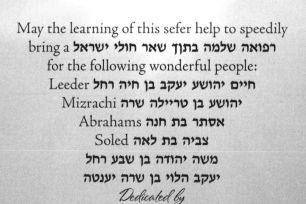

May the learning of this sefer help to speedily

bring a **רפואה שלמה בתוך שאר חולי ישראל**

for the following wonderful people:

חיים יהושע יעקב בן חיה רחל Leeder

יהושע בן טריילה שרה Mizrachi

אסתר בת חנה Abrahams

צביה בת לאה Soled

משה יהודה בן שבע רחל

יעקב הלוי בן שרה יענטה

Dedicated by

Rabbi Moshe Meir & Miriam Libby Weiss

Subscribe Today!

Receive a Torah tape or CD
from Rabbi Moshe Meir Weiss
every week!

To subscribe—write, call or email
with your name, address and phone number to:

Rabbi Moshe Meir Weiss
P.O. Box 140726, Staten Island, NY 10314
Tel: 718-983-7095 ✦ Email: rmmwsi@aol.com

For tape subscriptions:
$20 for one month ✦ $120 for 6 months
✦ $240 for a whole year

For CD subscriptions:
$26 for one month ✦ $156 for 6 months
✦ $312 for a whole year